CUBA

CUBA

THE LAND, THE HISTORY, THE PEOPLE, THE CULTURE

BY STEPHEN WILLIAMS

Running Press
Philadelphia, Pennsylvania

A FRIEDMAN GROUP BOOK

© 1994 by Michael Friedman Publishing Group, Inc.

9 8 7 6 5 4 3 2 1

Digit on the right indicates the number of this printing.

ISBN 1-56138-188-8

Library of Congress Cataloging-in-Publication Number 93-85508

Page 133: Reprinted with permission of Charles Scribner's Sons, an imprint of Macmillan Publishing Company, from TO HAVE AND HAVE NOT by Ernest Hemingway. Copyright 1934, 1937 by Ernest Hemingway. Copyrights renewed © 1962, 1965 by Mary Hemingway.

CUBA
The Land, The History, The People, The Culture
was prepared and produced by
Michael Friedman Publishing Group, Inc.
15 West 26th Street
New York, New York 10010

Editor: Nathaniel Marunas
Art Director: Jeff Batzli
Designer: Lynne Yeamans
Layout: Jan Melchior
Photography Editor: Susan Mettler

Photos on pages 2 and 6 © Marc PoKempner

Color Separations by Bright Arts (Hong Kong) Ltd.
Printed and bound in China by Leefung-Asco Printers Ltd.

This book may be ordered from the Publisher.
Please add $2.50 for postage and handling.
But try your bookstore first.

Running Press Book Publishers
125 South Twenty-second Street
Philadelphia, Pennsylvania 19103-4399

FOR RYAN WILLIAMS

I would like to thank

The Center for Cuban Studies in New York,

the photographer Peter Cunningham,

the writer Charles Bricker,

and my editor, Nathaniel Marunas,

for helping me complete this book.

And thanks to my many

friends in Cuba, who prefer

to remain anonymous.

CONTENTS

CHAPTER
one

CUBA BEFORE COLUMBUS

THIS STUNNING VIEW IS TYPICAL OF THE BEAUTIFUL BEACHES OF EASTERN CUBA.

Walking along the *malecón,* or "sea wall," in the lovely town of Baracoa, it is possible to get a sudden and startling glimpse deep into Cuba's past. A light brown, squared-off face with unusually straight eyes—different from the African and Spanish features that shape most Cubans—will pop into focus from a crowd of people. There is history in the face, a continuity that can only be passed down through the genes. This is the face of Cuba before Columbus arrived, rare evidence of Indian blood still extant after five hundred years of genocide and intermarriage. While there are no pure-blood native Indians left in Cuba, these genetic traces are a reminder of how rich and ancient Cuban culture is.

The Baracoans will proudly point out those who have Indian blood, calling them over to say "Look at this beautiful face." These same Baracoans will gaze across the shockingly aqua sea toward the jungle on the far side of the bay and say that this quaint town is where it all began. Even the name *Cuba* has roots in the language of the Indians who lived around Baracoa.

As with so much involving the conquest of the New World, there is a lot of dispute about how many Indians lived in Cuba before the conquest, but there were probably between 100,000 and 500,000 people in a variety of communities. The Spanish called the various groups by the name *Arahuacos,* or *Arawaks,* but there were at least three distinct groups: there is clear evidence that the *Guanajatabeys,* hunter-gatherers who lived in the area now called Pinar del Rio, in the western part of the island, were in Cuba at least as early as 3500 B.C.; the *Ciboney* arrived later, establishing themselves as fishermen and farmers along the southern coast; finally, there were the *Taíno,* who first visited by boat from what are now the Dominican Republic and Venezuela around A.D. 1100. The Taíno didn't really settle in significant numbers on the island until they were driven from their homelands by the cannibalistic Carib invaders just a century before Columbus laid eyes on the New World. An argument could be made that the Spanish were just the latest of the various peoples who had "discovered" Cuba, although no one can dispute that Columbus' arrival was to leave the most lasting impression.

The Spanish saw the Taíno as backward and godless; the natives' practice of inducing broad foreheads in newborns

National Museum of the American Indian Smithsonian Institution

DRESSED IN THEIR FINEST CLOTHES, THESE RURAL CUBANS POSE IN FRONT OF A BOHIO IN THE TOWN OF MONTECRISTI, IN 1916. THE BLOOD OF THE ORIGINAL CUBANS, THE TAINO AND CIBONEY, AS WELL AS OF THE AFRICAN SLAVES, CAN BE SEEN IN THEIR FEATURES.

by putting pressure on the infants' soft skulls certainly would have supported the former view. While most modern accounts describe the Indians as having lived peaceful and idyllic lives that were at odds with the unparalleled frenzy of greed for gold and other riches that drove the Spanish to conquer the island—even Columbus said the Taíno were "very free from wickedness"— the Taíno were not angels. There is evidence that when the Taíno arrived they enslaved the Ciboney and drove them to the western end of the island, away from their eastern homelands.

While the Indians lived a primitive life by our standards, even the masses in fifteenth-century Europe led very difficult lives that we would likewise see as lacking in the most basic amenities. In fact, the Taíno were very sophisticated. They lived in round thatched huts that were designed to hold up remarkably well during hurricanes; slept in cotton nets strung from poles or trees; paddled the rivers and sea in boats they made by burning and carving large tree trunks (Columbus later described these as being "all in one piece, and wonderfully made"); and during religious ceremonies smoked a broad leaf they cultivated.

The Taíno were skilled potters, turned cotton into cloth (the men went naked, but the women wore aprons), and ate a varied diet. Corn was the principal crop, and Columbus probably first saw this grain in Cuba. The Taíno word for corn was *mahis*, which the Spanish pronounced as *maiz*, and which in English is maize. Some of their foods, such as yucca (also called *manioc*, not to be confused with the spike-leafed plant common in desserts), yams, and peppers, are integral to modern Cuban cuisine. (Other treats, like turtles, iguanas, and snakes, aren't often found in smart Havana and Miami restaurants today.)

THIS FANCIFUL ENGRAVING PURPORTS TO SHOW A TAINO LEADER LECTURING COLUMBUS ABOUT THE IMMORTALITY OF THE SOUL. OLD ENGRAVINGS SUCH AS THIS ARE OFTEN BASED ON FANTASY: THE INDIANS ARE DEPICTED WITH EUROPEAN FEATURES AND THE CONQUERORS ARE INVARIABLY DRESSED MORE NATTILY THAN ONE WOULD EXPECT OF A CREW WHO HAD JUST CROSSED THE SEA IN A SMALL, CROWDED BOAT.

Taíno farming methods were advanced and ecologically minded so as to preserve the land and offer better yields. It has been estimated that the Taíno way of planting and harvesting produced more food with less effort than any farming methods used in Europe at that time.

Most villages were made up of about fifteen families governed by a *cacique*, or "clan leader." The villages sometimes formed alliances with other villages, but there is no record of any wars; one chronicler of the European conquest wrote that he never once saw the Taíno fighting among themselves. They were described as being remarkably kind; this might have been their undoing, because the record of the conquest shows a pattern of brutality and acquisitiveness on the invaders' part that is perhaps unmatched in the history of the world.

The following, from *The Conquest of Paradise*, by Patrick Sayle, is from Columbus' writings about the Taíno, whom the explorer encountered on various islands, including Cuba.

They are the best people in the world and above all the gentlest. . . . They became so much our friends that it was a marvel. . . . They traded and gave everything they had, with good will. . . .

I sent the ship's boat ashore for water, and they very willingly showed my people where the water was, and they themselves carried the full barrels to the boat, and took great delight in pleasing us. . . .

They are very gentle and without knowledge of what is evil; nor do they murder or steal. . . .

Your Highness may believe that in all the world there can be no better or gentler people . . . for neither better people nor land can there be. . . . All the people show the most singular loving behavior and they speak pleasantly. . . .

They love their neighbors as themselves, and they have the sweetest talk in the world, and are gentle and always laughing.

At least one contemporary Cuban historian has looked at the Taíno through a Marxist filter, calling them the first and purest socialists, because their society was one that spread the wealth around, shared property communally, and took care of its less fortunate members. While this may be an idyllic portrait, the Taíno certainly were living a life of plenty in tropical paradise when Columbus arrived. Columbus wrote the following of the Indians in Cuba.

It is certain, that among them, the land is as common as the sun and water; and the Mine and Thine (the seeds of all mischief) have no place with them. They are content with so little, that in so large a country, they have rather superfluity than scarceness. So that (as

we have said before) they seem to live in the golden world, without toil, living in open gardens, not entrenched with dikes, divided with hedges, or defended with walls. They deal truly one with another, without laws, without books, and without Judges. They take him for an evil and mischievous man who takes pleasure in doing hurt to others.

The extraordinarily beautiful archipelago these Indians named includes the 760-mile (1216km) -long main island (about the size of England), the *Isla de la Juventud*, or "Isle of Youth" (formerly *Isla de los Piños*, "Isle of Pines"), and about four thousand other small islands and keys. At its narrowest it is thirty-five miles (57km) wide and at its broadest, 198 miles (320km) wide. Three mountain ranges that cross Cuba, the Cordillera de los Organos, the Sierra del Escambray, and the Sierra Maestra, offer cool mountaintop climates. To a tropical people, these mountains, where the temperatures "plunge" at night to 50 to 40 degrees Fahrenheit (5–10°C), might as well be in Antarctica for all the shivering they induce. The valleys are made of rich soil that was perfect for the Indians' crops. Pure jungle rivers rush to the sea, filled with fish. And fetid, insect-infested swamps are home to all types of birds.

The forests are full of rich tropical fruits, animals, and the other necessities the Indians would have needed for a good life. Even today country people near Baracoa can walk a few hundred yards into the woods and find cacao, oranges, papaya, mango, coconut, and almonds to eat, fibers from which to weave cloth, and many other useful natural products. While there aren't many indigenous mammals (the Spanish thought one mammal, the large native manatee, or sea cow, was a mermaid), poisonous snakes, or large wild cats, there are many birds. There are also iguanas and *jutías* (large rodents that live in trees). The whole main island is surrounded by Caribbean and Atlantic waters that wash onto some of the most dramatically beautiful beaches in the world. The sand comes in white, black, or tan, all finely grained and clean.

This paradise had remained largely unchanged for thousands of years. When the Spanish fleet arrived, the Taíno greeted the explorers with offerings of fruits and other foods. Their generosity was not repaid in kind. Within ten years of Columbus' first visit, Cuba had completely changed: it was the property of a king who lived across the ocean; its native people were subject to strange laws and customs; and for the first time the land was opened to raw exploitation instead of prudent management.

Within one hundred years after Columbus made landfall, virtually every pure-blooded Indian had been murdered or had succumbed to diseases that the foreigners had brought along with guns, horses, and a lust for gold.

Archive Photos

THE VAST AND LUSH CUBAN FORESTS IMPRESSED COLUMBUS AND HIS MEN, BUT IT'S DOUBTFUL THAT THOSE FORESTS WERE AS OVERWHELMING AS THE JUNGLE THESE INDIANS ARE WALKING THROUGH.

≋ THE COMING OF COLUMBUS

Cuba was neither the first land Columbus sighted in the New World nor the most significant, but it ranks up there with the most misunderstood. On the first voyage, Columbus insisted that Cuba was not an island but rather was the mainland where the Indies began. He speculated that Cuba was the southern land point of Asia, beyond which would be the spices and riches and great civilization he had set out to find. Columbus took this notion very seriously. Some of his crew dismissed it, much to their subsequent chagrin.

When the crew speculated that Cuba might really be an island, and not the tip of the Indies, Columbus forced each and every one of them to swear that the land they had been sailing along for four weeks was the mainland. The penalty for saying anything to contradict the oath was a large fine and the removal of the offender's tongue. If your tongue was cut out for this heresy and somehow you still tried to insist that the land mass was an island, you were given a hundred lashes. The punishment for further obstinance was not recorded, but it is doubtful anyone pushed Columbus that far—how vocal could you be without a tongue?

Columbus was simply trying to justify his voyage so he wouldn't return to the king and queen of Spain a failure for not

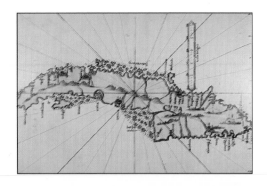

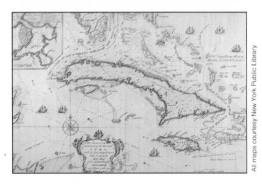

All maps courtesy New York Public Library

OLD MAPS OF CUBA WERE LEFT BY THE VARIOUS CULTURES THAT LEFT THEIR MARKS ON THE ISLAND, INCLUDING THE SPANISH (TOP), THE FRENCH (MIDDLE), AND THE ENGLISH (BOTTOM). THIS PORTRAIT OF CHRISTOPHER COLUMBUS (OPPOSITE PAGE) IS PURE FANTASY; NO AUTHENTICATED DEPICTIONS OF THE VISIONARY AND TEMPESTUOUS EXPLORER EXIST.

having found an overseas passage to the markets of India. After all, Cuba seemed long enough that it *could* be the continent. Why rock the boat?

Reality soon caught up with Columbus, however, and the Old World began its rush to the New World. Columbus made several more voyages across the Atlantic, and by 1506 a map by Contarini clearly showed Cuba as an island, though it wasn't circumnavigated until 1508, by the explorer Sebastián de Ocampo.

It wasn't long before the Spanish became preoccupied with finding gold in the New World. The Indians' jewelry showed that Cuba offered some gold, and the Indians themselves indicated there were great amounts of the metal on the island, but there didn't turn out to be much at all. The Indians shouldn't have tried to be such accommodating hosts. Certainly they underestimated the Spanish lust for gold and the consequences of letting those desires go unfulfilled. Many Indians were killed in the single-minded and largely fruitless search for the precious metal.

For the most part, Cuba was seen as a poor cousin of the nearby lands and was practically abandoned for a time in the years right after the conquest. At the same time, other islands in the area were being explored and exploited, their native cultures destroyed, and all their limited quantities of gold removed to the distant coffers of the kingdom of Spain.

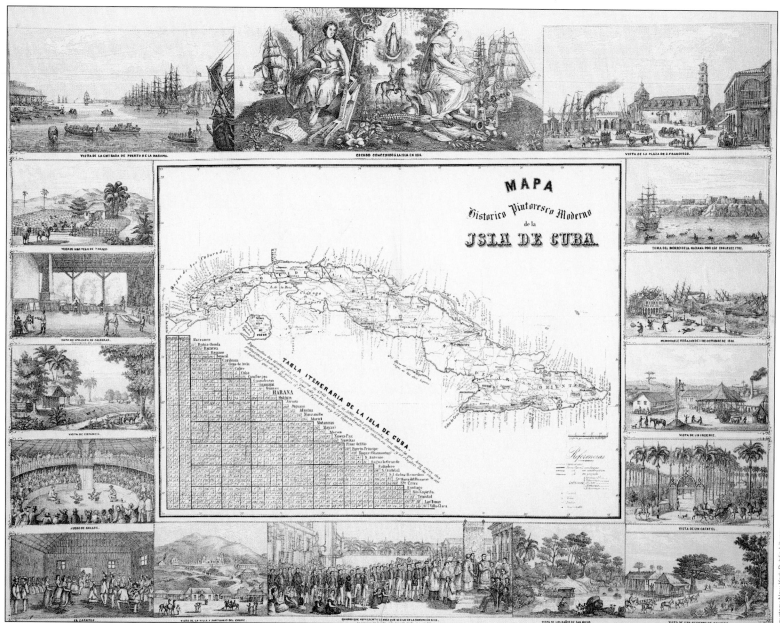

On his first voyage, Columbus touched land at various harbors along the northern coast of Cuba, and then on November 27, 1492, he dropped anchor in an almost perfectly protected harbor near the easternmost point of the island. He named the spot Puerto Santo. While almost everything about Columbus, including the points where he made landfall in Cuba, are in dispute, it isn't hard to believe that he landed in this harbor. The site can be located easily from Columbus' writings because he described a distinctive local mountain that Cubans now call El Yunque. *El Yunque* means "The Anvil," and this tall, flat-topped mountain is clearly visible from the harbor.

These days tourist bars serve a rum-and-coconut milk cocktail called El Yunque, and the name Puerto Santo is reserved for a modern luxury hotel at the spot where Columbus supposedly landed. Despite the ravages of time (and tourism), the place has not lost the exquisite tropical beauty that first impressed the Spanish.

Legend has it that on his first landfall in Baracoa, a stay that lasted seven days, Columbus left a wooden cross. According to the official historian for Baracoa, Dr. Alejandro Hartman Matos, who heads the Matachín Museum, Columbus left the cross upright in some rough stones at the entrance to the harbor in 1492, where it was found by later conquerors. Now, over five hundred

years later, it is on display in the Catholic church in Baracoa, overseen by Father Valentín Sanz, a young, bearded priest who helps keep the legend of Columbus alive in the town. You can enter the church and look at the dark, well-worn

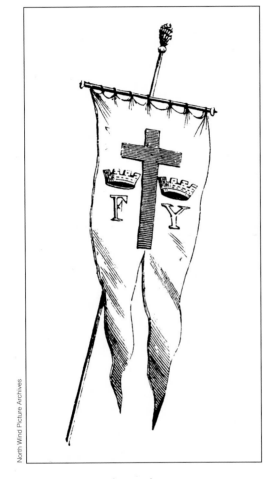

North Wind Picture Archives

THIS BANNER (ABOVE) WAS THE OFFICIAL LOGO OF COLUMBUS' FIRST EXPEDITION TO THE NEW WORLD. THIS LIVELY MAP (OPPOSITE PAGE) GIVES THE DISTANCES BETWEEN MAJOR CUBAN TOWNS AND OFFERS VIEWS OF TOURIST SIGHTS AND TYPICAL SCENES FROM CUBAN HISTORY.

cross that over the years has acquired silver ornamentation and a deep, rubbed luster, and get a strong sense of history. Columbus touched this cross, and if you are lucky, Padre Valentín will let you touch it, too.

Of course, modern skeptics have done their best to debunk the wonderful story of this small-town relic. They have examined the wood and compared it to hundreds of trees from around the world and concluded that the cross was made from wood local to Baracoa. So, say these experts, Columbus couldn't have brought the cross from the Old World to the New.

"Who says he did?" says Dr. Hartman Matos. "Why couldn't he have made it here and left it?"

"That would certainly make more sense," says Father Valentín.

And the case is closed.

Whether Columbus left the cross or not, it is a true relic of the early days of the Spanish occupation of Cuba. Few dispute that a conquistador found it in 1510, and that it is genuine. The cross has suffered various indignities through the years, including pirate raids on Baracoa and invasions of mercenaries trained in the United States, to name just two examples. But the cross continues to endure, a vivid reminder of the pivotal influence of the Spanish on the development of Cuban culture, and a symbol of the culture that conquered the Indians and made the island its own.

CHAPTER two

THE FOUR-HUNDRED-YEAR BATTLE

THIS FANCIFUL PORTRAYAL OF THE CAPTURE OF EL CANEY, EL PASO, AND THE FORTIFICATIONS OVERLOOKING SANTIAGO DE CUBA IS TYPICAL OF U.S. VERSIONS OF THE CONFLICT IN ITS FAILURE TO DEPICT ANY CUBANS AMONG THE ATTACKING FORCES.

In 1493, the Pope gave Spain control of all the lands that Columbus had found, and ordered that Christianity be taught to the Indians. According to this decree the Spanish were not supposed to take slaves. But they wanted slaves. They got around the prohibition by creating *encomiendas* (from the verb "to entrust"), plantations that used slave labor in the name of religious redemption. Under this ingenious system the colonists could capture Indians and force them to work, all the while maintaining that their imprisonment was only to teach them Christian ways.

The encomiendas were undeniably brutal. And because the Indians were only temporary wards of the Spanish— the colonists were supposed to free the Indians once they became Christians— the Spanish would work them especially hard, literally until they died, so as to get the most in exchange for the room and board and Bible study they provided.

At first there weren't many encomiendas in Cuba, because the other islands in the area were more important to the Spanish, but this didn't mean the Indians were spared. Various Spanish invaders explored the island and took Indians as *encomiendados* (the polite term for slaves) to work in the other Caribbean settlements. The Indians were no doubt surprised that these foreigners they had originally greeted so warmly were turning out to be so brutal. As more and more slave hunters invaded Cuba, the Indians quickly shed their pacifistic ways and began to fight the kidnappers with bows and arrows.

Because there was communication between the various islands near Cuba, the Cuban Indians learned of the violent means the invaders had used to subdue other islands, and in the first years prepared for what they expected would be an invasion on a mass scale. They were aided by an Indian warrior named Hatuey, who had battled the Spanish earlier on the island of Hispaniola (Haiti and the Dominican Republic), and fled to Cuba after being defeated. Hatuey hated the Spanish, whom he saw as covetous men in search of gold and the slaves to mine it who would take what they wanted at any cost.

The ferocity of the once-docile Indians of Cuba must have surprised Diego Velázquez de Cuellar when he landed in 1510 near what is now Guantánamo Bay, but it certainly didn't stop him. He and his men were prepared and hungry for battle. Among the army

IN THE INIMITABLY CRUEL STYLE OF THE MID-SIXTEENTH CENTURY THIS CATHOLIC PRIEST OFFERS THE INDIAN RESISTANCE LEADER HATUEY THE OPPORTUNITY TO SAVE HIS SOUL BEFORE HE IS ROASTED ALIVE. HATUEY, WHOSE NOBLE IMAGE HAS BEEN SO ABSORBED BY CUBAN CULTURE THAT IT NOW GRACES THE LABELS OF BEER BOTTLES ACROSS THE ISLAND, REFUSED TO ACCEPT THE EUROPEAN GOD.

of about three hundred was an ambitious man named Hernando Cortés, who would later sail out of Havana harbor to conquer the Aztecs in Mexico with a mixture of cleverness and only a small number of soldiers and horses.

From the moment Velázquez and his men arrived they were doing battle with Hatuey and his warriors, and the Indians were winning. The Spanish were eventually forced to retreat to a wooden fort, called Nuestra Señora de la Asunción (now the town of Baracoa), that had been built by earlier colonists. Hatuey held them under siege in this fort for three long months.

The Spanish conquistadores did not take over the entirety of South and Central America by brute force alone, however; cunning and planning were often the keys to their successful conquests, from the Incan empire to the Aztec empire. Cuba was no different. The entrapped Spaniards recognized that they didn't need to kill every last Indian soldier to end the siege, but rather only had to capture the heroic Indian Hatuey. And that is what they did, though they didn't just hold him prisoner; they publicly humiliated him and then burned him at the stake, a common tactic of the day.

Before dying, Hatuey was able to pull grace out of the fire. The Spanish gave him the chance to accept Christianity at the last moments before he was roasted. Hatuey turned down the opportunity, saying boldly that he did not want to spend eternity in any heaven that was filled with Christians.

Hatuey thus became Cuba's first martyr to independence, and he is lionized to this day. His image is memorialized throughout Cuba, especially by a proud statue in the center of Baracoa, not too far from a statue of Columbus, and the location of the first Spanish fort. Furthermore, his face appears in every bar and restaurant and at every wedding and fiesta in eastern Cuba— on the label of the wildly popular beer called, simply, Hatuey.

THE END OF THE INDIAN RESISTANCE

Though Hatuey lives on in memory, the Spaniards' methods were effective; the Indian army fell apart after its leader was martyred. There were subsequent rebellions and battles here and there, but the Indians never again had the unifying leader that any successful defense would have required. Hatuey's death marked the end of significant Indian resistance to the Spanish, and the end of the native island culture.

Velázquez forged across the island with his conquistadores, killing Indians or enslaving them to hunt for what little gold there was. Many Indians were beaten and tortured when the Spanish suspected them of keeping their gold deposits secret. Other Indians died from diseases (introduced by the Spanish) to

North Wind Picture Archives

which they had no natural immunity. (The Indians are said to have extracted their revenge in the form of syphilis, which quickly spread from the Americas throughout an unwary Europe.) Many thousands of Indians died or were murdered in this conquest.

According to witnesses, entire tribes of Indians killed themselves rather than face genocide, while others staged hit-and-run missions—the precursor to modern guerilla warfare—against the Spanish. These latter Indians were given the name *cimarrón*, which lives on in Cuban culture as a name for wildmen or runaways, and has even been used in Hollywood to describe the classic western hero.

One cimarrón chief named Guamá, along with his wife and sixty others, tormented the Spanish from the mountains near Santiago in the early 1550s with hit-and-run attacks, kidnappings, and murders until the rebel and his band were finally captured and killed. (The Castro government gave the chief's name to a modern Cuban resort built in the traditional thatched-hut Indian style over canals and streams; a buggy Venice in the swampland, the resort is designed to lure foreign tourists, including the Spanish, so the Cuban government can capture the valuable foreign currencies.)

In the end, Guamá's band was nothing more than an irritant to the brutal and greedy occupying army that felt its mission was sanctioned directly by God, via the Pope. By the time of Guamá's rebellion the Spaniards had spread across the entire island, and by the end of the rebellion the Indians' culture was almost extinct. By 1570 not a single pure Indian remained, and very little of the original culture survived— just the knowledge of how to make a few useful objects the Indians once used, such as hammocks and canoes, and some place names, including Cuba, the name with Indian roots that the conquistadores chose for the lovely island that was now completely theirs.

≋ SLAVE LABOR

The Spanish were very disappointed to discover that there wasn't much gold or silver in Cuba, especially considering the incredible amounts that were flowing out of South America and Mexico, but the island gained importance as the key to the New World, with good harbors that were convenient staging grounds for conquests and shipping ventures.

Because so many Indians died battling the Spanish or on the encomiendas from diseases and beatings and over-

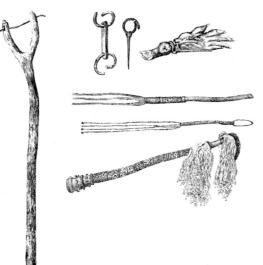

North Wind Picture Archives

work, slaves were brought in from West Africa to keep the riches flowing from the New World to the Old. The first record of slavery in Cuba is from 1513, when a man named Amador de Lares got permission to bring four Africans over from the neighboring island of Hispaniola. One of the first large groups of slaves was brought to Cuba in the 1520s, when three hundred prisoners began forced labor in a gold mine named Jaugua.

The African slave trade was regulated by the Spanish and Portuguese crowns, which at the time were unified, and many of the merchants were Portuguese. The business of selling humans was done on a huge scale: one trader, Gómez Reynel, was authorized to transport 4,500 Africans annually to the New World, mostly to the Antilles islands, including Cuba.

Unlike in North America, in Cuba the arriving Africans were allowed to stay in groups based on where they

---

THE COLONISTS TREATED THE WEST AFRICANS WHO WERE BROUGHT TO CUBA (AND THE REST OF THE CARIBBEAN) NO BETTER THAN THEY TREATED THEIR ANIMALS. SLAVE OWNERS HAD NO QUALMS WHEN IT CAME TO FORCING THE SLAVES TO DO THEIR BIDDING, AS ILLUSTRATED BY THESE TOOLS OF THE SLAVE TRADE.

came from, and were able to keep their languages, religions, and traditions alive. The slaves came largely from the Mandingo, Fulani, Hausa, Ibu, Ijo, and Yoruba people, all West African tribes with highly developed civilizations. They were not, as is often assumed, primitive peoples; in fact, these strong African cultures were to have a great influence on Cuban society over the centuries.

All romanticism should be put aside when it comes to thinking about slavery in Cuba, although the system there was in many ways less oppressive than in the United States. Slaves were allowed to

THE BRUTAL METHODS USED TO CAPTURE PEOPLE AND TRANSPORT THEM FROM THEIR HOMES IN WEST AFRICA TO SHIPS BOUND FOR THE CARIBBEAN WERE FUNDAMENTAL IN THE DEVELOPMENT OF THE ECONOMIES OF THE CARIBBEAN COLONIES. THE SPANISH SETTLERS DEPENDED ON THE SWEAT OF AFRICAN SLAVES TO TRANSFORM CUBA INTO A COMMERCIAL CENTER OF THE AMERICAS.

get married and have families, and could own and sell property and buy their freedom if they earned enough money. In addition, children born to a slave and a colonist were considered to be freemen. But generally, the living conditions for slaves were abysmal. The Spanish built towers several stories tall to watch over these humans that were worked like farm animals, cutting sugar cane all day long in the oppressively hot sugar fields. One tower still stands outside of Trinidad, a solemn and beautifully constructed testament to the brutality and ingenuity of the Spaniards. From these

North Wind Picture Archives

HORRIBLY CROWDED QUARTERS, LACK OF FOOD, AND SHORTAGES OF FRESH WATER MEANT THAT MANY SLAVES DIED DURING THE LONG OCEAN VOYAGE FROM WEST AFRICA TO THE CARIBBEAN. THEIR BODIES WERE UNCEREMONIOUSLY DUMPED OVERBOARD.

towers a single man could watch over hundreds of acres of sugar cane, keeping an eye on productivity. At night the slaves were kept in barracks.

The very nature of slavery meant that it was destined to become a major source of problems for the Spanish in Cuba, especially when African slaves and freemen became the majority in the country. In 1532 slaves revolted in Cuba for the first of many times, at the Jobabo mine, and a few years later slaves in Havana sacked the city amid the chaos following an attack by French pirates. This was only the beginning. Over the centuries slaves and their descendants were to figure prominently in fights for independence from the Spanish.

By the middle of the sixteenth century, the conquest of the Americas had become institutionalized and the Spanish were taking everything of value that they could find from the newly conquered lands. With this bounty of emeralds, gold, silver, and other riches pouring out of the Incan empire of Peru and the Aztec empire of Mexico, Cuba took on greater importance as a staging ground for the Spanish empire. Because it is located at the mouth of the Gulf of Mexico, on the main route (including the overland passage across the isthmus of Panama) from Peru and Mexico to Europe, Cuba soon became the hub of Caribbean shipping and trade.

Velázquez founded what are still known in Cuba as the seven villas, the colonial towns of Baracoa, Santiago de Cuba, Bayamo, Puerto Príncipe (now called Camagüey), Sancti Spíritus, Trinidad, and San Cristóbal de la Habana. Some of these towns, especially Trinidad, still retain their colonial presence. Even today you can walk past charming, colorful buildings in Trinidad on streets paved with cobblestones that had served as ballast in Spanish ships coming to pick up riches from the New World.

⬟ PIRACY IN THE CARIBBEAN

By 1526 all ships carrying gold and silver were required by royal decree to return to Spain in convoys to avoid pirates, who had begun to roam the Caribbean in alarming numbers. The crown received one fifth of all the loot that came out of the Americas, and wanted these ships to travel safely. The money was needed to pay for Spain's war with France and to stop Protestantism from creeping across the continent towards the Iberian peninsula. And aside from wars and politics, Spain hungered for the influence that the astounding sums leaving the Americas had on the economic structure of all of Europe. So the convoys, which at times included as many as ninety ships that gathered in Havana harbor over a period of months to prepare for the voyage to Spain, were extremely important. Forts were built in Havana to protect the loot.

THE HISTORIC CENTER OF TRINIDAD RISES GRANDLY FROM THE MORE CHAOTIC NEIGHBORHOODS THAT SURROUND IT. COBBLESTONE STREETS AND HOUSES WITH WINDOWS GUARDED BY WOODEN *REJAS* EVOKE EARLIER CENTURIES. TRINIDAD IS A TOURIST'S DELIGHT, WITH WONDERFUL OLD BUILDINGS AND MUSEUMS.

© Marc PoKempner

THE BUILDINGS IN TRINIDAD REFLECT THE STYLES OF SEVERAL CENTURIES, AND MANY HAVE BEEN RESTORED BY THE CUBAN GOVERNMENT, WITH THE HELP OF THE UNITED NATIONS. SOME STREETS ARE STILL PAVED WITH COBBLESTONES THAT WERE BROUGHT OVER AS BALLAST ON SHIPS FROM EUROPE.

All the fortification of the day couldn't keep the pirates away. One particularly vexing type of pirate was the French corsair. In those years there was no international maritime law, and nations would actually raid each other's ships. Furthermore, because France and Spain were enemies, the French encouraged corsairs, or state-sanctioned pirates, to attack and loot Spanish ships—as long as they gave a percentage of the booty to the French crown.

There were many corsair attacks. In 1521, Giovanni da Verrazano, a Florentine pirate working for the French, looted a ship laden with Aztec treasures. In 1522, Jean Florin took a shipment of gold Cortés was shipping to Charles V. In 1537, French corsairs attacked the island itself, raiding two ships in Havana harbor that were laden with Mexican treasures. The worst attack came the next year, when corsairs led by Jacques de Sores took Havana by surprise and found very little opposition. They drove most of the people out of the city and demanded money from the Spanish crown before they would leave. The governor, Gonzalo Pérez de Angulo, decided to retake the city, and attacked with forty Spaniards, one hundred Africans, and one hundred Indians. Although they killed twenty-five of the French, the governor and his followers were driven back. Sores' retaliation was brutal: he executed scores of prisoners, among them men, women, and children. Then he demanded even more money. When it didn't arrive, he burned Havana to the ground. He sold some slaves in the city and hanged the others, leaving their bodies to rot in the sun. The brutality was fueled in part by the fact that many of the pirates were Huguenots, happy to get revenge on Charles I of Spain for his religious persecutions.

By this time Spain had claimed complete trading and colonization rights to the New World, but its power was to be challenged again and again. By the mid-fifteenth century England had emerged as a strong naval force, and the two countries became great rivals. Not surprisingly, England wanted more access to the new market.

In 1567 an Englishman named John Hawkins showed up in Veracruz, Mexico, trying to sell some slaves, in violation of Spanish charters. The Spanish attacked and sank two of his three ships, but Hawkins escaped on the third, which was captained by Sir Francis Drake. (Drake was the first Englishman to circumnavigate the world, plundering South America and returning to London a rich man.) Drake and others continued to challenge Spanish dominance in the Americas over the years. In 1585, Drake arrived in the Caribbean with twenty-five ships and two thousand men and pillaged Cartagena (now in Colombia) and Santo Domingo (now in the Dominican Republic), and then acted as if he were going to attack Havana, though he refrained. Still, the threat of invasion drove the Spanish to build more forts to protect the city.

The piracy continued, reaching a peak in the 1630s, when Dutch pirates began to join the French and English. In the early 1600s, the Dutch Admiral Piet Heyn assembled three thousand men and thirty-one ships to wait for the fleet coming out of Veracruz. They captured and looted all the ships, securing huge amounts of gold, sugar, indigo, and silver.

The Caribbean was by now a nest of pirates, and they were the biggest problem facing Cuban cities. Santiago de Cuba was sacked in 1662, and Sancti Spíritus in 1665. There were four hundred raids from 1665 to 1666 on Cuba alone. And no place was safe: given the narrowness of the island, the pirates thought nothing of attacking towns in the middle of the country. Piracy was to continue well into the nineteenth century, at times disrupting the economy and halting all sugar and tobacco trading.

≋ THE SEEDS OF REVOLT

While all this was happening, the population of Cuba wasn't growing as dramatically as elsewhere in the Americas, because the commercial focus was on places like the silver mines of Potosí, Bolivia, and the mountains outside of what is now Mexico City. In the seventeenth century the population of Cuba barely doubled.

When a new royal family took over Spain at the beginning of the eighteenth century, Cuba began to be more sophisticated and more heavily populated. This period in Cuba is notable for the education and cultural life the crown encouraged. By 1760 there were more people in Havana than in New York, Boston, or Philadelphia. The first secondary school was built in the early 1700s. The first printing press started in 1720. The University of Havana was built in 1728.

By 1734 Cuba had a police force. The first newspaper was published in 1763. The next year, Cuba established a national postal system that eventually served all the Americas. The Royal Seminary opened in 1769. A public library was established in 1793. Many monuments and parks were built in Havana. Streets were paved. A promenade was built along the harbor. The first theater, Teatro Tacón, was built; it is now the oldest theater in operation in the Western hemisphere. Cuba was becoming wealthy—and ready for revolution.

Still, the Bourbon throne did not bring enlightenment to Cuba. In 1740, about forty thousand, or just under one fourth, of the people in Cuba were slaves. The throne encouraged trade, but often had such tight controls that too much of the profits went directly to Spain and too little went to the tobacco and sugar producers. There were several revolts under the Bourbons.

In 1717 the tobacco growers, or *vegueros*, in Havana who had less access to the black market than other growers on the island (because the Spanish kept tighter control on Havana) rose up against the Spanish and were defeated. They tried again a few years later, even burning the fields of growers who cooperated with the crown. Some of the insurrectionists were killed, and they failed to break the Spanish monopoly. The old system of controlled prices and black market profiteering remained.

☰ THE GROWTH OF AN ISLAND

Troubles in Europe influenced events in the Americas, and several times in the eighteenth century Spain and England were on opposite sides. In 1762, with Spain and England at war in Europe, the English navy assembled the largest force seen in the New World up to that time: two hundred boats and 22,000 men. With plans to take Havana, they landed in the village of Cojimar (which Ernest Hemingway later used as the setting for *The Old Man and the Sea*), and then attacked El Morro, the fortress that to this day guards Havana harbor. The city was defended by only nine thousand men, including slaves who had been promised their freedom in return for fighting, but still the siege lasted for two months. The English finally took control on August 12, 1762.

The British opened Havana up to free trade and the economy grew at an astounding rate. Slaves and goods from Europe and Africa arrived and sugar and tobacco left in a frenzy of trade among the North American colonies and the countries of Europe.

After only a year in Havana the British traded their Cuban possessions to the Spanish for what is now the state of Florida. Wisely, the Spanish didn't try to return to the same tight system of controls after the British left. Not too much later, after the colonies declared

Cuba-Havana-Morro Castle From Punta Fortress

Cuba-Havana - The Fortress

-Havana-Morro Castle

WHILE TODAY THERE WOULD BE AN OIL TANKER OR A RUSSIAN CARGO SHIP ON THE WATER INSTEAD OF A SAILING VESSEL, THESE VIEWS OF EL MORRO, AT THE ENTRANCE TO HAVANA HARBOR, HAVE CHANGED LITTLE OVER THE YEARS.

themselves independent, North American traders began doing business directly with the Cubans. Up until this time Cuba hadn't had much of a market for its sugar, but the colonists' collective sweet tooth was to have a profound effect on the sugar trade.

The sugar plantations grew in number and size to satisfy the North American craving, and the resulting increase in the number of slaves was to change the face of Cuba permanently, affecting its racial makeup, its religious traditions, its art and music, and its economy—modern Cuban culture is as African as it is Spanish because of the influence of slaves and their descendants. And the new wealth created by the trade with the colonies—a wealth that wasn't all spirited to Spain, as it had been in the past—changed the face of Havana, as people built many of the distinctive and beautiful colonial houses that still stand as monuments to the past.

The North American influence wasn't only economic. The American Revolution inspired great desires for freedom from Spain among the Cuban-born Spanish and *criollos* (people of mixed Spanish and African descent). Copies of Thomas Paine's *The Rights of Man* and the U.S. Declaration of Independence were secretly passed around Cuba by hand, out of sight of agents of the crown.

The French Revolution, which followed fifteen years later, only added to the liberation itch. For almost two centuries the criollos had watched all the riches of the Americas leave and cross the ocean to Spain. And the criollos, feeling perhaps more Cuban than Spanish by this time, wanted their share of the economic and political power.

It was also at about this time that people in the United States, which at the time was buying 40 percent of its sugar from Cuba, started to make noises about possibly making the island a part of the union.

MASTER AND MAN

In 1791, the neighboring island of Saint Domingue (now called Haiti) experienced a revolution, and the slaves became the rulers, casting off the French colonists. Rather than submit to the political will of their former slaves, the French elite of Saint Domingue, many of them sugar plantation owners and coffee growers, fled the island. About thirty thousand of them came to Cuba, bringing their superior knowledge of sugar production with them. (The French influence in architecture is still very much in evidence in Havana and Santiago and other Cuban towns.) This exodus changed the economy of the Caribbean, making Cuba vastly more important and powerful, and leaving Saint Domingue essentially without a sugar industry.

These added plantations required even more slaves as Cuba replaced Haiti as the dominant sugar producer in the Caribbean. In the fifteen years following the arrival of the French, 91,000 slaves officially passed into Cuba, with countless more undocumented slaves being imported illegally. As the slave culture grew and the landowners and sugar refiners got richer, the lives of the slaves got proportionately worse.

As startling an effect as the number of incoming slaves had on Cuba, the true boom in slavery and sugar production didn't take place until the years 1821 to 1831, when over 600,000 slaves were put to work in Cuba. The slaves came from Bantu, Mandingo, Dahoman, Congolese, and Yoruban tribes. By 1823 these blacks outnumbered whites in Cuba, and they weren't happy with their lot in life. Many tried to flee; others plotted revolts. Runaway slaves gathered in bands in the mountains and were given the same name given to Guamá and his group of Indians a century before: cimarrón. Their villages were called *palenques*.

There was also a fairly large group of blacks who either were free by birth or who had purchased their freedom, who lived around Cuba—especially in Havana. One of these men, José Antonio Aponte, plotted an insurrection to overthrow the institution of slavery in 1812, but his plans were uncovered and he was hanged by the Spanish along with some of the people who had helped him. The Spanish were particularly brutal towards Aponte, out of fear that his rebellion would grow. They beheaded him and left the head in a cage outside of his house in Havana for everyone to look at; they also chopped off one of his hands and nailed it to a wall along the street. Still, as time passed, the criollos and the Cuban-born Spanish began to side with the slaves against the royalists.

A CALL FOR REFORM

The early nineteenth century saw the decline of Spanish dominance in the Americas. The crown was weakened by its battles with France and England, and the Spanish monarch, Charles IV, was an ineffectual ruler. (For a time Spain was basically run by his wife's lover, Manuel de Godoy.) Furthermore, most countries in Latin America were fighting for independence from Spanish rule in the early years of the century. But Cuba remained loyal—for several reasons.

One reason for Cuban loyalty was that under the early eighteenth-century governor, Luis de Las Casas, the economy boomed. Spain was preoccupied with European wars and didn't have time to meddle as much in Cuban affairs, and Las Casas' policy of free trade opened up many markets. The economy grew tremendously and sugar prices went up. Another reason was that unlike the rest of Latin America, Cuba had no groups of unsatisfied Indians who wanted freedom (although African slaves soon filled this role). In fact, with the tremendous number of immigrants arriving from all over it was hard for any group to gain enough influence to really cause problems. There were various political groups: loyalists; reformists, who wanted changes in Spanish rule; separatists, who wanted total independence; and annexationists, who wanted to join the United States. Not surprisingly, these groups couldn't organize a unified front.

The annexationists were, of course, encouraged by the U.S. government. With the Louisiana purchase of 1803 granting the mouth of the Mississippi to the United States, that river became the principal point of entry and exit to the Gulf of Mexico for the middle territories of the United States. With Cuba lying so strategically at the mouth of the gulf, the U.S. government adopted the policy that no hostile power would ever be allowed to control Cuba.

Thomas Jefferson thought the easiest way to prevent this would be to annex Cuba for the United States. Thinking of the island's strategic importance, Jefferson wrote at one point: "I have ever looked on Cuba as the most interesting addition which could ever be made to our system of states." In 1808 he tried to get the Spanish to sell Cuba, but they declined. At least four other presidents eventually tried to buy the island from the Spanish, but were rebuffed. Nonetheless, North Americans continually hoped to acquire the land

that John Quincy Adams described as a fruit that would ripen until it broke off and fell into the lap of the United States.

By 1825, all the countries in Latin America were independent of Spain, except for Puerto Rico and Cuba. Despite this freedom movement, which seemed to mirror the U.S. fight for

© FPG International

THE UNITED STATES BECAME INTERESTED IN CONTROLLING CUBA EARLY ON. THOMAS JEFFERSON WAS THE FIRST OF SEVERAL U.S. PRESIDENTS TO TRY TO CAJOLE THE SPANISH GOVERNMENT INTO SELLING THE ISLAND, WHICH HE THOUGHT WOULD MAKE A NICE TROPICAL ADDITION TO THE UNITED STATES.

autonomy a half-century earlier, the U.S. government did not want to see a free and independent Cuba. First of all, few officials believed the Cubans were capable of taking care of themselves, given their history. And, perhaps more importantly for many of the citizens of the United States, which still had a lucrative system of slave exploitation in place, many feared that an independent Cuba would be ruled by blacks, which might eventually lead to problems for the southern slave states.

The independence and emancipation movement in Cuba, however, had a mind of its own. In the early 1840s slaves rebelled in Matanzas, an area that still boasts huge fields of sugarcane, and were brutally put down. Rumors spread throughout Cuba that a cross-section of the people was preparing to fight the government for self-rule. In response, the Spanish, never known for their subtlety when it came to negotiation in the Americas, began a period of violence unprecedented in Cuba that is now called *La Escalera*—"the staircase" or "ladder"—after one of the innovative forms of punishment employed. (An estimated four thousand people, mostly black, were lashed to ladders and whipped into confessing that they were rebels, or failing that, whipped until they died.) Hundreds perished. A few thousand others were imprisoned. The criollos, always happy to christen a martyr, found one in the poet Gabriel de la Concepción Valdés, commonly called Plácido, who was killed because his poetry was critical of tyranny.

The Spanish maintained control with this round of repression, but officially abolished the slave trade the following year, perhaps to prevent future violence. Nonetheless, the slaves were not liberated, and the law turned out to be cosmetic. After the 1850s, a more organized independence movement started, and the constant warfare that had plagued Cuba since Columbus arrived was to continue.

≋ A CALL TO ARMS

Cuba's history has been marked by numerous peculiar invasions carried out by every kind of invader, from swashbuckling pirates to the bumbling exiles trained by the CIA. One of the more improbable invasions was led by Narciso López, a Venezuelan who was perhaps inspired by Simón Bolívar's attempts to liberate countries in South America.

López sought out and found financial backers in the United States for an invasion of Cuba. The U.S. investors no doubt felt that an independent Cuba would want to join the United States, and saw great business opportunities in this outcome. A fighting force of five hundred men was recruited from Kentucky and Mississippi to spark a revolt in Cuba. Gauging the dissatisfaction of the island's people, López had

"LA BAYAMESA"

The Cuban national anthem, "La Bayamesa," was composed following the Mambí victory at Bayamo. While the Spanish soldiers soon forced the Mambí to retreat, the song lived on.

Run to combat, men of Bayamo
may the motherland be proud of you.
Don't fear a glorious death,
for to die for the motherland is to live.
To live in chains is to live
under shame and indignity.
Hear the clarion call,
to your arms, brave ones, run!

Don't fear the ferocious Spaniards,
they are cowards, whose total tyranny
can't resist the brave Cuban;
their empire will fall forever.
Think of our triumphs,
think of them as fallen;
because they were cowards they
ran away beaten,
Because we are brave we know
how to triumph!
We can shout Free Cuba!
with the terrible explosion
of the cannon,
listen to the clarion call.
To your arms, brave men, run!

decided that the population would rise up against the Spanish at the tiniest opportunity.

In 1850, López's invaders landed near Cárdenas, in what is now the popular resort area called Veradero, to get things going. Visionary though he might have been, however, López didn't seem to have been much for micromanagement. Although the mercenary soldiers

were united by a purpose (lust for money), they were divided by language. Hardly any of the soldiers spoke a word of Spanish, and López and his Hungarian assistant, General Pragay, spoke very little English.

The Cubans weren't too impressed with this ragtag fighting force. In fact, instead of spontaneously rising up against the government when the invaders arrived, the citizens of Cárdenas ran to their houses and locked themselves in—after notifying the Spanish officials of the invaders' arrival. López and his men fled back to Key West before having to fight any significant battles.

López was not a quitter. He returned a year later with four hundred more soldiers and, presumably, a translator or two. Many of his soldiers were captured and executed by firing squads, including the nephew of the governor of Kentucky. This inflamed the North American press, which spread its fire to the public, some of whom called for an all-out invasion of Cuba.

Though López was stopped both times, his actions somehow encouraged the spirits of the criollos and slaves, and by the late 1860s there was a serious rebel movement forming in the eastern mountains. These mountains have always played an important role in Cuban revolutionary movements, including Fidel Castro's, and to this day the Cuban government thinks of the *oriente* as being an area that doesn't respect authority.

THE TEN YEARS' WAR

On October 10, 1868, a large eastern plantation owner named Carlos Manuel de Céspedes, who is still revered in Cuba as a great liberator, freed the slaves on La Demajagua, his plantation near Manzanillo, and demanded the emancipation of all slaves in Cuba. His declaration, known as the *Grito de Yara*, "Shout of Yara," started the Ten Years' War, which is remembered as the bloodiest period in Cuban history. He began a rebellion against the Spanish with only thirty-seven men, but this slave-owner, poet, lawyer, and rancher quickly inspired other plantation owners, many of whom had suffered severe losses during the collapse of the sugar market, to free their slaves and join the movement. Many of the former slaves and other small landowners from the east also joined the fight for independence, so it was a mixed army of blacks, mulattoes, and whites. The Spanish called them the *Mambí*, which in the Congolese spoken by the slaves meant "despicable and dirty." Within a week, Céspedes had gathered fifteen hundred men to his side. The first great battle of the war was for Bayamo, and it fell quickly to the Mambí, who wore white *guayabaras* and red scarves in their victory parade. (The song that would later become the Cuban national anthem, "La Bayamesa," was composed here after this battle.) But the celebration was short-lived; the Spanish

Gen. ANTONIO MACEO.

Courtesy New York Public Library

ANTONIO MACEO AND HIS TEN BROTHERS, DESCENDANTS OF SLAVES, GAVE THEIR LIVES TRYING TO FREE CUBA. HE WAS A TIRELESS LEADER IN THE TEN YEARS' WAR (OPPOSITE PAGE), AND LATER STUNNED THE SPANISH FORCES WHEN HE FOUGHT HIS WAY ACROSS THE COUNTRY.

quickly returned to retake the town. Instead of conceding defeat the Mambí burned Bayamo to the ground.

This led to an incredible reprisal in Havana and elsewhere, when Spanish loyalists burned Mambí sympathizers' homes and businesses, driving many of them out of the country. In a foreshadowing of what would happen when Castro took power one hundred years later, at least 100,000 Cubans left the island in 1869, many for the United States. All their lands were appropriated and given to the loyalists.

José Martí y Perez, who would eventually become the most revered of Cuba's pantheon of heroes, was arrested for the first time during this purge, after the authorities found a note he had written to a schoolmate saying he supported the revolution. The teenage Martí was sentenced to six years hard labor, breaking stones. He was released from his sentence early, in 1871, on the condition that he go into exile in Spain.

The U.S. government's official response to the bloody war was that it wanted the Cubans and Spanish to resolve their differences with treaties. And while sympathetic North Americans supplied a great deal of money to the rebel movement, the U.S. government never recognized the legitimacy of the rebels, again because it did not really want to see a liberated Cuba under black rule. Hamilton Fish Armstrong, the Secretary of State under President Grant, went so far as to say that a mixed-blood country of Africans and Spanish such as Cuba wouldn't be able to self-govern successfully. The best solution as far as Armstrong and others were concerned would be for the

Historical Pictures/Stock Montage, Inc.

Spanish to get sick of fighting and make an offer to sell the island to the United States. For the United States, the war was seen almost as a negotiating tactic in a huge real estate deal, but the deal didn't quite turn out the way the United States wanted.

In 1869 Céspedes drew up the first Cuban constitution and the rebel assembly elected him president. The fighting continued, with the Spanish offering a stiff defense against the rebel forces.

Many civilians were killed and the economy was destroyed. In 1873 Céspedes was killed in battle, after having been deposed by his own troops.

Finally, after ten bloody years, in which about 250,000 Cubans and 80,000 Spaniards died, the Cuban government offered the rebels a general amnesty in return for their surrender. The rebels, with one major exception in Antonio Maceo, agreed. The Pact of Zanjón was signed in 1878, with Spain giving the island some limited independence by changing it from a colony to a more-or-less self-governing protectorate. The pact included many reforms, such as direct representation for Cubans and freedom for all slaves who had fought with the rebels. However, nothing really changed. Despite the horrendous destruction and suffering it had gone through, the country was hardly more independent at the end of the war than it had been at the beginning.

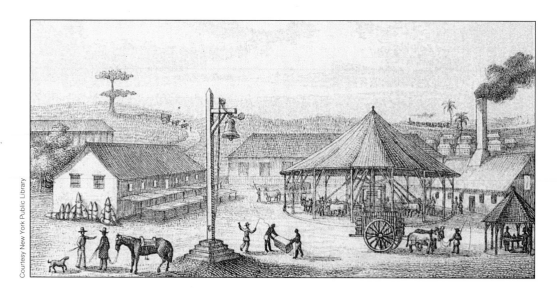

Courtesy New York Public Library

BEFORE THE ADVENT OF STEAM ENGINES, SUGAR CANE WAS PRESSED WITH THE AID OF SLAVES AND OXEN, AS IN THE ILLUSTRATION ABOVE. BELOW, THE LADIES OF THE *INGENIO* ARE SERVED REFRESHMENTS AS SLAVES BOIL MOLASSES IN THE BACKGROUND.

Courtesy New York Public Library

Many North American investors took advantage of the chaos following the war by buying up huge tracts of abandoned or unused land at very low prices. The war had severely damaged the Cuban economy, especially the tobacco industry; the only industry that remained strong was sugar growing and processing. While the mills were owned mostly by Spaniards and Cubans, most of the trade was done with the United States. After the war, U.S. companies invested a lot of money—some say as much as $100 million—in gaining control of and upgrading the processing plants.

While slavery was finally abolished in 1880, blacks didn't start to live free lives. Instead of chains, they were shackled by poverty and misery. The labor was still done as it had been done in the past, only now the slaves were free men—free to be brutally exploited by the colonial system that so many people in Latin America, led by Bolívar and others, had struggled to overthrow. Yet another war for independence seemed inevitable.

≋ MARTÍ

José Martí y Perez, the boy who had been imprisoned at the age of sixteen for writing a note, became an agitating exile from his base overseas. He received a law degree in Spain, then lived in France, Mexico, and Guatemala before returning to Cuba for a short time. He was driven by a burning desire to help Cuba to free itself of its colonial status. The government soon exiled him again to silence his dissent. Establishing himself in Cuban exile communities in New York and Florida, Martí wrote journalism, poetry, and philosophy that heralded the coming liberation of his country. He wrote many articles that were published in the powerful North American and Latin American newspa-

Courtesy New York Public Library

JOSE MARTI IS WITHOUT DOUBT THE MOST REVERED FIGURE IN CUBAN HISTORY, AND HIS NAME HAS BEEN APPROPRIATED FOR USE IN PROPAGANDA BY EVERYONE FROM FIDEL CASTRO TO THE FIERCELY ANTICOMMUNIST EXILES IN MIAMI. EVEN THE U.S. GOVERNMENT RADIO STATION THAT BEAMS YANQUI NEWS TO THE SOCIALISTAS BEARS THE NAME RADIO MARTI.

pers of the day. Martí called the period following the Ten Years' War a "time of fervent repose," as the liberationists regrouped and reorganized to make another attempt to free their country.

Martí organized Cubans in the United States, including the Cuban Revolutionary Party (CRP), which was made up of exiles in New York and cigar makers in Florida, and tried to convince the North American public to support Cuban independence. The only requirement for membership in the CRP was the desire to overthrow the government in Cuba and create a government that didn't discriminate by race. Martí desired more than just independence from Spain; he wanted a country based on social justice and fair economic practices.

Martí feared the idea of manifest destiny that was gaining such credence at this time because he didn't want the United States to dominate a liberated Cuba. Exemplifying the dialectical relationship that exists between the two countries to this day, he raised money in the United States to finance a revolution that he hoped would deny U.S. power and influence in Cuba. After some difficulties with the U.S. government about whether or not he could ship supplies to the island, he was finally able to lead the CRP in an uprising against the Spanish in 1895. Martí and the first six thousand rebels landed in several places in eastern Cuba in February of that year. Sadly, Martí, who was responsible for this fight for freedom, was the first casualty of the day during fighting in Dos Rios in May. His death only elevated his stature in the eyes of the Cuban people.

Martí is a potent symbol of liberation, and his name is praised and used by all sides in propaganda. Under Castro, pictures of Martí and quotations from his writings are displayed all over the country. Cuban schoolchildren study Martí and win Martí awards for doing well. And at the same time the anti-Castro radio station in Florida financed by the U.S. government to help encourage revolt against Castro's government is called, what else, Radio Martí.

Though Martí was dead, his cause was carried on by Máximo Gómez and the black radical Antonio Maceo, who had fought valiantly to the end of the Ten Years' War. Maceo and his ten brothers all would eventually give their lives to the independence of Cuba, but not before building an army of over sixty thousand soldiers. Maceo and Gómez marched across Cuba from the eastern tip to Pinar del Rio in the west, shocking the Spanish with their victories. The rebels had their greatest successes with guerilla tactics, although once in a while they fought traditional battles with the loyalists and won. The war, as with so much of Cuban history, was brutal and harmful to the civilian population.

The Spanish governor, Valeriano Weyler, responded to the rebels with one of the most vicious campaigns ever launched in Cuba. Called the *reconcentración*, this involved forcing nearly everyone who lived in the country, peasants and villagers alike, to vacate their land. Those who refused were killed. Many others died en route. Thousands starved to death. And countless civilians were killed by bullets, machetes, and other violent means.

President William McKinley, who had seen the horrors of the American Civil War firsthand as a soldier for the Union army, refused to send troops to Cuba to quell the incredible destruction, even though there was a lot of popular support for the Cubans among U.S. citizens. Cuban exiles offered money and other materials to support the rebels—some even tithed their wages to support the revolution. The reports of the rebels' struggles for independence touched a chord in North Americans, who saw in the Cuban struggle shades of their own distant war for independence from the British.

Finally, after hearing endless reports of atrocities at the hands of the Spanish, McKinley gave Spain a warning to end the war once and for all. He started secret negotiations to get Spain to sell Cuba to the United States. This sale would, of course, end the war. More significantly, it would give the United States the island it had been coveting for over a century. That the new ownership would be couched in terms of liberation and peace was all the better.

≋ THE SPANISH-AMERICAN WAR

Spain refused to grant Cuba freedom or sell the country to the United States, but offered concessions to the rebels, which indicated that Spain felt its side was losing. Instead of accepting, the rebels wisely continued fighting and the country fell into complete chaos. The United States, spotting an opportune time to intervene and gain influence on the island, responded to riots in Havana by calling in a warship, the *Maine,* supposedly to protect North American citizens living there. It blew up and sank in the harbor, killing 258 people, most of them Americans. At the time the official line was that the ship had been blown up by a bomb, and the United States blamed Spain. Other theorists have accused the United States of blowing up its own ship to justify an invasion and annexation of Cuba. These days it is generally accepted that something in the ship's engine caused the explosion. Still, the United States was up in arms and the press, fueled by William Randolph Hearst and his newspapers, went crazy.

The United States hadn't fought in a foreign country in fifty years; the Civil War had been over for more than three decades; and the modern navy that had been put together in the 1880s and 1890s had yet to be tested. So there were a lot of young North Americans itching to test their mettle in Cuba.

On April 25, 1898, the Spanish-American war began. The war wasn't confined to Cuba, but included engagements with the Spanish in the Philippines—they were subdued in one day—and Guam and Puerto Rico. The North American public was certain the country was doing the right thing, in large part because of what was being printed in the papers, especially those owned by Hearst. His papers played up the horrors to the extreme, describing Cuba as nothing more than an incredible bloodbath, with Spanish soldiers raping and pillaging their way across the island. Hearst used this "splendid little war," as he called it, to boost the circulation of his papers. "Remember the *Maine*" was the battle cry of the U.S. soldiers.

The United States justified its war with the Spanish as a way to liberate the suffering Cubans, but not all Cubans were so sure that the splendid little war was so necessary. Many felt that within a year they would have been able to eject the Spanish without help. The revolutionaries didn't want the United States to join the fray, fearing the advent of a new colonial power. Martí was dead, but his warning to his countrymen was very much alive: "The road must be blocked that leads to the annexation of the peoples of our America by the angry and brutal North which despises us; we are flooding that road with our own blood . . . . I lived inside the monster and I know its entrails."

"REMEMBER THE *MAINE*" WAS THE BATTLE CRY OF THE UNITED STATES IN ITS STRUGGLES WITH SPAIN IN CUBA, PUERTO RICO, AND THE PHILIPPINES. U.S. TROOPS CHEERED THEIR VICTORY AT SANTIAGO DE CUBA, BUT ARROGANTLY NEGLECTED TO INVITE THE CUBANS TO THE CELEBRATION, EVEN THOUGH THE CUBANS HAD BEEN FIGHTING THE SPANISH FOR YEARS.

U.S. OCCUPATION

To appease the Cubans the U.S. Congress added the Teller Amendment to its declaration of war. This said that the United States did not want to control Cuba, but to restore peace. The amendment, however, was merely a smokescreen to placate the rebels. It was written broadly so as to be meaningless in terms of keeping the United States from its goal of becoming the de facto ruler of Cuba after the war, and it didn't take the rebels long to figure this out. The independence fighters joined the U.S. Navy to block the harbor at Santiago de Cuba, but after that the Cubans were shunted into the background. The North Americans didn't think too much of the Cuban independence fighters, who had been fighting heroically for years and had almost defeated the Spanish without any outside help. The North Americans thought the Cubans were dirty and ragged. Besides which, many of the Cubans were black or of mixed race. Stephen Crane, a reporter for both Joseph Pulitzer's and Randolph Hearst's papers, called the Cubans "a collection of real tropic savages."

Even before the troops arrived in Cuba, the U.S. command had decided that the Cubans wouldn't help in the fighting, but would instead be put to work doing manual work behind the scenes. The Cubans, of course, after years of beating down the Spanish, didn't think this was right, and General Garcia refused to make his men do this kind of menial work.

This racism caused a lot of problems between the Cubans and the North Americans, especially after the Cubans weren't given credit for their heroics at the most major land battle of the Spanish-American war in Cuba, the taking of San Juan Hill, which cost fifteen hundred Cuban and North American lives. These days the battle of San Juan Hill isn't thought to have been quite as heroic as it was originally made out to be (it is also thought that Teddy Roosevelt was on foot, rather than on a white horse). At the time, however, a great fuss was made over this charge up San Juan, and the newspapers portrayed Theodore Roosevelt and the Rough Riders as folk heroes. Typically, the Cuban involvement in this pivotal confrontation was largely ignored, and little credit was given to the heroic Mambí.

When the Spanish surrendered Santiago, on July 17, 1898, the Mambí were not invited to the victory parade or the ceremony. They were forbidden even to enter the city and were ordered to surrender their weapons. This was an incredible affront by an occupying force to a valiant army that had sought independence and was now facing yet another foreign occupation. By the new year a new flag flew over Havana: the stars and stripes of the United States.

More than three years followed during which time the U.S. military ruled Cuba; and the representatives of North American interests on the island hoped that Cuba would sooner or later ask to be admitted to the Union. The U.S. public did not unanimously approve of this new imperialism, which included U.S. control of other former Spanish holdings of Guam and Puerto Rico. Some leading Americans said it went against the principles of the country; others took the more racist attitude that the dark-skinned people in these countries could only hurt North America if they became part of the Union; and others just felt imperialism was wrong. Though the landowners and businessmen in Cuba favored U.S. control, the Cuban people wanted independence.

Before too long the United States made a point of giving Cuba its freedom, but at the end of a short leash.

In 1901 Cuba adopted a new constitution, but it was far from a complete and satisfactory victory for the independence fighters. This constitution had been written in Washington, and included something called the Platt Amendment, which gave the United States the right to intervene in Cuba whenever it felt such action to be necessary. This amendment also gave the United States the privilege of having naval bases on Cuba, which explains the U.S. presence at Guantánamo to this day. When the Cuban congress expressed its

dissatisfaction with the new constitution, the occupying leader, Army General Leonard Wood, said he and his troops would remain in Cuba until they changed their minds.

In 1902 Cuba's first elected president, Tomás Estrada Palma, took power. He was the first in a series of U.S. puppets. The modern era had begun.

In a departing gesture, the United States allowed Cuba to change the U.S.

U.S. TROOPS CHEERED THEIR VICTORY AT **SANTIAGO DE CUBA**, BUT ARROGANTLY NEGLECTED TO INVITE THE **CUBANS** TO THE CELEBRATION, EVEN THOUGH THE REBELS HAD BEEN FIGHTING THE **SPANISH** FOR YEARS.

flag for the modern Cuban flag (perhaps because the designer of the Cuban flag, Narciso López, based the blue and white stripes, red triangle, and white star on the Texas flag). But symbolism wasn't enough for many people. The heroic Máximo Gomez lamented having fought so hard and having seen so many die for so little independence. "It's not the republic we dreamed of," he said of the new Cuba.

CHAPTER three

GANGSTERS AND DICTATORS

THE BEAUTIFUL BAY OF PIGS WAS THE SETTING FOR THE UNITED STATES' ILL-ADVISED INVASION OF APRIL 1961.

uba won the war against Spain, but instead of independence the island got a new master. The four centuries of rigid authority under the Spanish was replaced by a more modern, and more insidious, colonization by the United States. The Cubans were allowed to use their own flag and to choose their own leaders (most of the time) but Uncle Sam was never far from view. When Washington spoke, the Cuban government listened.

Almost twenty years of warfare had ruined the country's economy, and incredible amounts of North American money flowed into Cuba as investors saw the opportunity to build an influential beachhead. North Americans took over at least three quarters of the Cuban sugar industry, whereas before the war U.S. interests had controlled only 15 percent. These investors bought land, cigar factories, and railroads, and there was a construction boom that changed the face of Havana.

All this money was good for the country, and enabled the upper classes to prosper in the coming years, but there were few benefits for the descendants of slaves and country people who had fought so valiantly for independence. The rich got richer, and the poor just kept struggling to survive.

The demand for Cuban sugar grew as the sugar-beet fields of Europe were idled by World War I, and the prices the sugar barons received for processed cane skyrocketed. A tide of money rolled into Cuba, and Havana took on a new luster that began to make the island the jewel of the Caribbean once again. Many of the plush mansions, with their grand marble staircases and crystal chandeliers, that still make Cuba such a romantic place were built with this sugar money. Enrique Caruso performed in Havana. Bars, nightclubs, race tracks, and casinos opened everywhere. Rich men came to Havana from all over the world for long, booze-filled evenings and escapades with beautiful Cuban women.

As the forces of morality came down hard in the United States in the twenties and alcohol was banned, Cuba

THIS POSTCARD WAS MAILED FROM HAVANA'S HOTEL PLAZA TO WEST ORANGE, NEW JERSEY, ON JUNE 29, 1935. THE PLAZA STILL STANDS, REMODELED AND FILLED WITH FOREIGN TOURISTS, A LIVING REMINDER OF CUBA'S DECADENT PAST.

Archive Photos

became even more attractive. Tourists flocked to the island, taking daily boats over from Miami and Key West to spend decadent vacations in Havana carousing in casinos, dance halls, brothels, and luxury hotels. The city was so openly promiscuous that at least one downtown doctor's office hung a sign advertising cures for *enfermedades venereas: sifilis*.

After a series of presidents who kowtowed to the interests of the United States, an extremely independent though uniquely corrupt man named Gerardo Machado was elected to lead Cuba in 1925. His government was especially susceptible to *la mordida*, or "the bite," where a palmful of dollars or pesos would buy government favor or make a policeman momentarily see no evil, do no evil, and hear no evil. This denigration of the laws did much to hurt the already poor masses of Cuba, and helped fill the pockets of the Machado family.

By now sugar prices had plunged, and the worldwide depression had come to Cuba. A North American photographer named Walker Evans arrived in this milieu early in the summer of 1933 to

IN THE EARLY TWENTIETH CENTURY TOURISTS FLOCKED TO CUBA FOR THE SOPHISTICATED NIGHTCLUBS AND RESORTS, BLIND TO THE PROBLEMS THAT PLAGUED THE COUNTRY—CORRUPTION, STATE VIOLENCE, AND POVERTY.

THIS PHOTOGRAPH BY WALKER
EVANS CAPTURES THE ARCHETYPAL
WORLD VIEW OF THE DEBONAIR
CUBAN OF THE 1930S: SMOOTH, SLIM,
AND IMPECCABLY DRESSED.

document Havana. His book *Havana
1933* offers a brilliant portrait of a country teetering on the edge of violent revolution amid the corruption and poverty
and tropical splendor that has always
made Cuba such a compelling place. *A
Farewell to Arms* was playing in the movie
theaters and Ernest Hemingway was
carousing around town, staying at his
home-away-from-home, the Ambos
Mundos hotel in the historic heart of
old Havana. One can't help but wonder
how much Hemingway helped Evans gain
access to some of the more sordid sights
pictured in *Havana 1933*. Certainly
Evans did a remarkable job of capturing
the heart of the city, and Hemingway,
who had lived in Havana for years and
was much revered in the country, must
have been an insightful guide.

Evans' publisher hadn't given him
enough money to complete his assign-
ment, so Hemingway footed the bill
for a final week of drinking and taking
photographs in the rapidly collapsing
paradise that was Havana. The black-
and-white photos show the range of
Cuban society, from a prosperous-look-
ing black man in a sparkling white suit

and straw hat, who fits the image the world still has of the dashing Cuban, to a woman looking out from behind the woven palm fronds that form the doorway of her ghetto home. There are wealthy people walking the streets in their finest clothes, a man sleeping off a drunk on a bench, and a poor, dirty family eating fruit in front of a palatial home.

≋ DANGEROUS DESPOTS

As the economy worsened, opposition to Machado became more obvious and threatening. A man named Julio Antonio Mella founded the first Communist Party in Cuba and led strikes in the cities and even took over sugar mills and plantations in the countryside. There was rioting across the country, especially in Havana, where violence and tension created a fatal atmosphere.

As had been the case time after time since Columbus arrived in Cuba, the government wasted no time discussing humanitarian responses to the protest. Machado got right down to business in a bloody campaign waged against the opposition. He closed universities, made public meetings illegal, and quieted students, journalists, and union leaders by having them assassinated. Mella fled to Mexico only to be murdered on foreign soil by Machado's forces.

The fury of the population, however, proved too great for Machado. Late in the summer of 1933 a general strike

across the nation forced the dictator to flee the country in a plane, sporting five revolvers and carrying a bag full of gold.

After Machado there was great confusion in the country, which had descended into lawlessness. By this point a Cuban might have been forgiven for

looking back into history and concluding that the prospect of just government on the island was hopeless. (That person would probably have the same thoughts today: from the Spanish to Castro, Cuba has always had harsh rulers, most of them born of a revolutionary or missionary fervor that has been used to justify violent and oppressive rule. Benevolence doesn't seem to be part of the Cuban political vocabulary.)

A leader rose out of this chaotic mess who was destined to have a profound effect on the future of Cuba. Sergeant Fulgencio Batista staged a coup

A PAINED-LOOKING PRESIDENT RAMON GRAU SAN MARTIN STANDS IN A WHITE LINEN SUIT NEXT TO THE BOISTEROUS COLONEL FULGENCIA BATISTA.

within the military, and within a week had eliminated most of the old-regime officers and replaced them with soldiers loyal to him. He gave himself the title of Colonel Batista and eventually put his support (and the entire army) behind Ramón Grau San Martín, who believed he could do a better job of governing than the rulers he had replaced.

The problem was Franklin Roosevelt, president of Cuba's large friend to the north. In a foreshadowing of the Cold War, which was to have a profound effect on Cuba in the coming decades, Roosevelt decided that Grau's proposed workman's compensation law and desire for partial control over the electric rates charged by a United States–owned company indicated clear communist tendencies. (Strangely enough, the Cuban Communist Party thought the opposite, and accused Grau of being too far in the Yanqui court.) Of course, the United States has never appreciated communist tendencies, especially in the leader of a country less than ninety miles from the mainland.

In a gesture very similar to that made by Kennedy toward Castro twenty-five years later, Roosevelt flatly stated that the United States would not recognize Grau's government, and would never accept it, no matter how long Grau was president. Unfortunately for Grau, Colonel Batista, who basically had given Grau all the power the president held, didn't see the value of getting into a conflict with the United States over this issue. In a series of political moves Batista removed Grau as president and chose Colonel Carlos Mendieta to run the country. There is no doubt that the pragmatic Batista saw this show of fidelity to U.S. desires as an insurance policy on his power. He was not disappointed.

Various puppets ran the country for the next several years, but Batista was always backstage pulling the strings with his heavy hands. Batista was not, as he is often portrayed, just a boot-licking servant of the Americans. He was a man of African and Spanish ancestry who won the loyalty of many Cubans, and not just by force. Under Batista and his minions, the Cuban labor movement became very powerful, and a new forward-thinking constitution was adopted. Cuba actually became more independent under his rule.

In 1940 Batista himself ran for president and won a four-year term. At the end of that time he picked a man to succeed him, confidently predicting that the man would win the next presidential race. Remarkably, in the next election Batista's candidate was rejected by the voters in favor of none other than Ramón Grau San Martín, the president Batista had deposed just a decade before. Disgusted, Batista retired to Daytona Beach, Florida, and left his country in the hands of the man Roosevelt had called a red.

Far from being a communist president bent on bringing relief to the Cuban masses, however, Grau turned out to be just another in the long line of corrupt Cuban leaders. He brought incredible hardship and disillusionment to the Cuban people, including the young Fidel Castro. Grau's election proved to be the end of hope for the liberating powers of democracy in Cuba.

Grau was followed in the presidency by one of his gang, Carlos Prío Socarrás, who was elected in 1948. Not surprisingly, the government continued to be corrupt and the people continued to mistrust it. Then, in 1952, Batista returned to Cuba—just months before a general election—and put his hat in the ring. But before the election, which he had a very good chance of winning, Batista got jittery and used an army coup to regain power. Though no one knew it at the time, this coup was to have a profound effect on the history of the world. If the election had been allowed to proceed democratically, perhaps one of the greatest struggles of the Cold War would have been avoided: one of the reform-minded candidates for congress who saw his ambitions dashed when Batista canceled the vote was a young lawyer with a predilection for baseball and stylish suits named Fidel Castro.

Had Batista not staged the coup he might have been elected president, and Castro might have been elected to the congress, and later to the senate, and maybe even to the presidency. But fate would not have it that way.

≋ SIN IN THE SUN

Cuba's reputation as a tropical paradise where morality and responsibility were not required of foreigners grew in the following years. Most of the visitors, like tourists everywhere, were more concerned with having a good time than with bothering to think about the harsh day-to-day realities the average Cuban faced. The tourists would shop all day, gamble into the night, and then perhaps stop off at Friteria China for a special

Cuban spiced beef *frita* before heading back to their luxurious hotels.

A promotional magazine of the day describes Havana's nights of magic.

Close your eyes and visualize this scene: Night—a magical night with sky a velvety midnight blue scattered with a thousand glittering stars; low in the east the moon, incredibly large and golden.

A warm breeze tantalizingly scented with the intoxicating perfume of strange, exotic tropical flowers.

Music, warm sensuous, entrancing with Latin rhythms which set the blood to stirring and the feet to tapping.

Glamorous, lissome Latin lasses, black-eyed señoritas, languorously, enticingly swaying as they glide over a polished floor in a smooth rumba.

The bright excitement of gaming tables, the whir of the roulette wheel, the age-old chant of the croupier.

A dream you say? A dream that only the rich man can make come true?

How wrong you are!

This is the night-time in Havana . . . the "Paris of the Americas."

The Sybaritic temptations were everywhere. Cubana Airlines had flights direct from New York to paradise, which featured near-naked dancing girls high-stepping it up the aisle and exotic cocktails. The Sans Souci casino in Havana advertised itself with a scantily clad girl riding a donkey laden with bananas and

tropical flowers. Near the airport the Casa Marina catered to outlandish sexual fetishes, offering men without specific needs an array of Cuban beauties. It was common for high rollers in Miami to tell their families in the morning that they were going to be working late and then catch a flight to Havana for a day of gam-

THE TROPICANA DANCERS (ABOVE), CIRCA 1956. BAILERINAS STILL DANCE UNDER THE HAVANA MOONLIGHT, BUT THE OLD CASINOS (BELOW) WERE SHUT DOWN IN THE FIRST YEARS FOLLOWING THE 1958 REVOLUTION.

Archive Photos

"TO THE FOREIGNER"
BY JOSÉ MARTI

I destroy sheet after sheet of paper:
Pen strokes, advice, rages, and wild
    letters
That look like swords. What I write
I smudge, out of compassion, because
    the crime,
The crime is, after all, that of my
    brothers.
I run away from me, shake from the sun.
I would like
To know where moles dig their burrows,
Where snakes hide their scales,
Where traitors throw down their
    burdens,
Where there is no honor, only ashes.
There, but only there, I might be able
    to say
What they are saying and living: my
    country thinks of joining the
    barbarous foreigner!

JOSE MARTI WOULD HAVE APPRECIATED THE DEATH OF SLOPPY JOE'S, WHICH CATERED TO TOURISTS, SAILORS, AND HUSTLERS FROM AROUND THE GLOBE. THERE IS NOTHING LEFT OF THE FAMOUS BAR EXCEPT MEMORIES CLOUDED BY ALCOHOL AND THE NAME "SLOPPY JOE'S" WRITTEN IN TILE ON A FILTHY SIDEWALK IN FRONT OF A SHUTTERED AND DECREPIT HAVANA BUILDING.

bling and a visit to Casa Marina, only to return the same evening. Or maybe they would stick around an extra hour or two to pay a visit to the nightclub where "Superman," a Cuban whom nature had very generously endowed, displayed his marvels in the buff. For visitors, the atmosphere of Havana got freer and freer during the fifties, and this added to the city's allure.

The streets of Havana still, after more than three decades of communism and a blockade of Cuba, have tiles in the streets marking many of the restaurants

THIS IS A 1937 PHOTO OF FULGENCIO BATISTA AT HIS DESK. WHETHER OFFICIALLY IN POWER OR OPERATING BEHIND THE SCENES, BATISTA RAN THE GOVERNMENT OF CUBA OFF AND ON FOR MUCH OF THREE DECADES.

and shops once favored by tourists from the United States. While these places are now closed, their memory lives on in sidewalk names like Sloppy Joe's, which was a favorite of sailors and vacationers seeking a good time, and the various Woolworth Five and Dimes. (Their slogan was "Main Street is Woolworth's street in every important city in Cuba.") Cubans had United States–style super-

markets and movie theaters, and to this day you see well-preserved American automobiles of the 1950s tooling along Cuban roads.

The United States in turn was a major vacation, and even permanent, destination for Cubans. The concentration of Cubans in South Florida goes back to a time long before the Castro revolution, to the nineteenth century. Many American cultural influences have long been strong in Cuba, including baseball, which is the Cuban national sport. The positive side of the American influence on Cuba is the cultural interaction that developed, and this has led to a sort of love-hate relationship, which persists to this day. Most Cubans now have at least one relative who lives in the United States, and knowledge of North American culture is widespread. Much of the resentment Cubans now feel toward U.S. policies is counterbalanced by how close the two cultures are on the more basic, personal level.

≋ BATISTA'S SECOND "TERM"

During his second period of rule over Cuba, Batista proved to be a changed man, with little of the good sense and benevolence he had shown in his first term as dictator. He came back from Florida with more passion for the good life, and less interest in the little man. It seemed at times that he was running the country from the poolside or the gaming tables. He outlawed the communist party and openly courted the rabidly anti-communist U.S. Secretary of State, John Foster Dulles. This toadying up to the United States was deeply offensive to many Cubans, who to this day remain intensely nationalistic. Of course, they didn't dare to criticize Batista. Dissent was not welcome; Batista's secret police

MEYER LANSKY REVIVED HIS CRIMINAL CAREER IN THE WELCOMING ENVIRON-MENT OF CUBA AFTER HE WAS FORCED OUT OF BUSINESS IN THE UNITED STATES. HE EVEN TRIED TO WORK OUT A DEAL WITH FIDEL CASTRO AFTER THE REVOLUTION, BUT THE SOCIALIST AND THE SWINDLER DIDN'T SEE EYE-TO-EYE.

assassinated and tortured people who caused trouble for the regime, going so far as hanging them from trees in Havana.

Organized crime, represented by Meyer Lansky, gained a strong foothold in the tourist industry. Bribes were accepted by many in the government, including Batista. It was said that the slot machines around the perimeter of some casinos were never touched by casino employees. Rather, they were serviced by Cubans who came in from the out-side and took out the money, which ended up in the bank account of a mem-ber of Batista's close family. Gangsters were able to buy hotels and casinos in Havana (as long as some of the money ended up in Batista's purse), and the city's reputation as a den of immorality grew. The Cuban people began to see that not much had changed from the awful governments of Grau and Prío.

In the early fifties the *Saturday Evening Post* investigated the scene and said they could only find two honest places to gamble in Havana. One was under the grandstand of a race track, where locals would wager, and the other was the Montmartre casino, owned by Lansky. In those days Cuban casinos would rent space to entrepreneurs, who would run wickedly crooked games with the only limit to their profits being their own daring. So, curiously, the arrival of U.S. criminals meant more honest gam-bling. These professionals knew that you had to offer some chance of winning if

you wanted to draw in the high rollers. Lansky, with Batista's approval, cleaned up gambling in sin city and made it respectable again for visiting politicians, movie stars, and regular joes.

Lansky was pivotal in the redevelop-ment of Havana as a glamorous gambling spot (rivaled at the time only by Beirut). Lansky's Riviera hotel was a marvel of modern design when it was constructed in the late 1950s. The first major building in Cuba to have central air conditioning, it also boasted an egg-shaped, gold-leafed casino facing the Malecón and the sea beyond. Lanksy owned the whole operation, but in order to evade both the law and taxes he was listed only as the kitchen manager. Strangely enough, he took his title seriously, and even had Wolfie Cohen, of the famous deli-catessen Wolfie's in Miami Beach, teach him a thing or two. The customers in the luxurious dining rooms of the Riviera were not disappointed by the food, or by the view through the windows that opened onto the sea and the city. But only the wealthy could enjoy this splendor; just behind the Riviera there were poor Cubans living in shacks and on the sidewalk.

During Batista's reign the disparity between the wealthy and the poor only grew greater. About one fourth of all Cubans lived in poverty so severe as to be hard to imagine. They had no water, no sewage, no access to education or medical care. For peasants in the country, work was limited by the duration of the sugar cane harvest to about half the year. Yet at the same time the small number of wealthy people lived extravagant lives in the cities.

≋ BIRTH OF THE REVOLUTION

One year after Batista took power and began this violent and corrupt second period of rule, Fidel Castro—still smarting from having had his election to congress stolen out from under him—and about 125 others attacked an army post in Santiago de Cuba, hoping to spark a popular revolt that would drive Batista from power. They left the Granja Siboney, a modest farm outside of town where they had hidden cars and munitions in tobacco sheds, and proceeded to Moncada barracks (some of the rebels relying on commercial taxis) under cover of darkness and the music and dancing of *Carnaval*, which had consumed the city. The shell marks and bullet holes are visible to this day on the walls of Moncada barracks, but the attack failed. The survivors, including Castro, took off for the mountains.

Though the army had orders to shoot Castro on sight, he was fortunate enough to be captured after a few days by a sympathetic policeman. The policeman, instead of taking Castro to the barracks prison where he most certainly would have been killed in retaliation for the attack, took the revolutionary to the police jail. Public pressure, especially in eastern Cuba (where the people have always been quick to disagree with the government), was so great that Batista couldn't risk having Castro assassinated in the local jail, so he was put on trial. Acting as his own lawyer, Castro was sentenced to fifteen years in a prison on the Isle of Pines. He boosted his public standing at this trial by remaining defiant and independent, and in his closing words he spoke the famous line "Condemn me if you will. History will absolve me!"

The tough Isle of Pines prison was the pinnacle of modern penal design of the time, having been modeled on the federal penitentiary in Joliet, Illinois. But Castro had his own cell and plenty of books and used his time to study and become the firebrand he is today. It was here that Castro planned the revolution that was to bring him to power. It wasn't long before he was able to begin fighting again; after only two years he was released from prison—Cubans and people from other countries had demanded amnesty for him—and exiled. The occasion of the release was Mother's Day. Batista lived to regret his generosity, however, and later probably wished he had just sent a card.

CASTRO USED THE TIME HE WAS INCARCERATED IN THIS PRISON ON THE ISLE OF PINES (NOW CALLED THE ISLE OF YOUTH) TO PLAN HIS NEXT REVOLUTION. APPARENTLY HIS CELLBLOCK WAS CONDUCIVE TO THOUGHT, BECAUSE SOON AFTER HIS RELEASE HE STARTED HIS SECOND, AND SUCCESSFUL, WAR AGAINST BATISTA.

⧉ A CHARISMATIC REVOLUTIONARY JOINS THE FIGHT

While the revolutionary movement that put Fidel in power is called the M-26 (*Movimiento 26*) after the date of the attack on the Moncada barracks, that assault was really just a rehearsal for what was to follow. In Mexico, Castro met an Argentinian doctor, Ernesto "Che" Guevara, who was to become the mysterious figurehead of the revolution. Guevara was the poetic, charismatic philosopher of liberation who not only helped ignite the Cuban people, but sparked revolutionary movements all over the world. After training in Mexico under a retired Spanish Republican Army general, these two men and eighty others boarded a boat called the *Granma*, which had been purchased from an American in Texas. (The American had named his boat after his grandmother, though it is doubtful Castro knew the meaning of the word—the communist party newspaper today is also named *Granma*, and the boat is proudly displayed, encased in glass, outside the Museum of the Revolution in Havana.) After braving stormy seas they landed in Cuba on December 2, 1956.

Before the revolutionaries could do any damage to the government, Batista's troops killed or captured most of the invaders. Of the eighty-two original revolutionaries, only about a dozen sur-

vived. While the Batista government immediately started claiming that Castro had been killed, the truth was that he hid for several days in a field of high sugar cane as Batista's troops swarmed near him. Eventually he and Che and the others got together and made their way into the Sierra Maestra mountains outside of Santiago de Cuba, where Castro had hidden after the Moncada attack.

Although they were warriors for the common people, Castro and Che had a sophisticated grasp of public relations. To prove that the M-26 was strong, the revolutionaries smuggled in Herbert Mathews, a reporter for *The New York Times*, to interview Castro.

© AP/Wide World Photos

FIDEL CASTRO (ABOVE, CENTER) AND ERNESTO "CHE" GUEVARA (BELOW, CENTER) WERE INSPIRED REVOLUTIONARIES. CHE LEFT CUBA IN THE EARLY 1960S TO FOMENT REVOLUTION IN SOUTH AMERICA, AND IS BELIEVED TO HAVE DIED IN BOLIVIA.

Archive Photos

Archive Photos

A YOUTHFUL-LOOKING FIDEL CASTRO SMOKES A ROUGH, COUNTRY CIGAR. THESE DAYS HIS HAIR IS STREAKED WITH GRAY AND HE NO LONGER SMOKES CIGARS (HE QUIT SOME YEARS AGO AFTER WHAT HE CALLED A "HEROIC STRUGGLE"). THE CITIZENS WHO ONCE IDOLIZED HIM AS A FEARLESS PROPONENT OF THEIR RIGHTS NOW SOMETIMES CALL HIM "GRANDFATHER," HALF OUT OF AFFECTION, AND HALF OUT OF EXASPERATION WITH THE PACE OF CHANGE ON THE ISLAND.

Castro arranged for various rebels to come in and interrupt his conversation with Mathews to ask questions about what to do with various columns of troops that were nearby, so the reporter would get the impression that the rebel army was much larger than it actually was. The ploy worked, and the strength of M-26 was greatly exaggerated in news reports, befuddling the opposition. This reporter was to continue to give Castro very favorable press over the course of the revolution, and his stories in *The Times* helped to shape the world's romantic image of the struggle in Cuba.

At another point the rebels tried to smuggle the famous writer Graham Greene into the mountains. The author flew from Havana with a suitcase full of supplies for the guerillas, hoping that airport security wouldn't bother to check

HERBERT MATHEWS (BELOW, LEFT), A REPORTER FOR *THE NEW YORK TIMES*,
WENT INTO THE MOUNTAINS OF EASTERN CUBA TO INTERVIEW CASTRO AT THE
START OF THE REVOLUTION. MATHEWS' COVERAGE OF THE WAR
GENERATED A LOT OF SYMPATHY FOR THE REBELS, AND CASTRO SAW
THE PROPAGANDA AS VITAL TO THE GROWTH OF HIS MOVEMENT.

This page: © AP/Wide World Photos Opposite page: © Marc Pokempner

and even within the ranks there was incredible disloyalty. In addition, the army's battle plans were often disorganized and wrongheaded, especially when compared to the orderly movements of the strictly disciplined and zealous revolutionary army.

The Cuban revolution was amazingly nonviolent. The rebels had several serendipitous victories against Batista's troops, and with immense popular support from Cubans who had been waiting half a century for their liberation to truly take place, Castro led his troops toward power. Batista reacted with more intense repression, arresting and torturing people thought to be sympathetic to the revolution, often leaving their bodies in public places as a warning to others. But the warnings were too little and too late for Batista; almost everyone in Cuba now opposed him and his brutal tactics.

〰 NEW YEAR'S DAY, 1959

During the day of December 31, 1958, wealthy tourists and gamblers relaxed on chaise lounges near the swimming pools of the gigantic Hotel Nacional, the Habana Hilton, and the other luxury palaces, enjoying the strong Cuban sun. Over at the Riviera, Lansky and his staff were preparing for a big New Year's Eve blowout. As the day progressed the Riviera staff was surprised to receive hundreds of cancellations for its big

the bags of a distinguished Englishman. Greene was never able to make contact with the fighters up in the mountains, but the suitcase was delivered. Although Greene and Castro never made contact, Greene's experiences in Cuba were strong enough to inform his book *Our Man in Havana*. Furthermore, Greene remained a vocal supporter of the Cuban revolution for years.

This not only boosted Castro's international standing, it also caused a flood of young Cubans to leave the cities and farms and join up with the rebels. Still, there were never enough rebel soldiers to equal Batista's army. What made the difference was the tremendous popular support for the rebels and their charismatic leaders, Fidel and Che. Batista's troops represented repression,

THE HOTEL NACIONAL SERVED AS A LUXURIOUS HOME-AWAY-FROM-HOME FOR MOVIE STARS, GANGSTERS
AND POLITICIANS UP UNTIL THE REVOLUTION. WITHIN A FEW MONTHS AFTER CASTRO'S VICTORY, HOWEVER,
THE TOURISTS BEGAN TO STAY AWAY. THE GAMING ROOMS CLOSED. THE DECADENCE DISAPPEARED.

show. That night the casino and hotel were strangely quiet. At one o'clock in the morning, just when the streets should have been filled with drunken revelers, Batista responded to an offer from President Dwight Eisenhower and fled Cuba with his family in three jets commandeered from the Cuban air force. In the great tradition of Cuban leaders, he took his fortune with him to Florida.

At dawn, people were dancing in the streets of cities across Cuba. The music coming over the radio included the song "Mamá, Son de la Loma" ("Mama, they're from the hills," in reference to the new leaders of Cuba). In a demonstration of anti-Batista fervor, people beheaded hundreds of parking meters all over Havana. (The Batista regime had said publicly all along that the money from the meters was to be used to feed the poor, but everyone always knew that the change was going into the pockets of Batista's close family.)

The workers at the Riviera walked off their jobs to celebrate Batista's fall. Lansky ended up in the kitchen cooking for the startled guests. His wife, Teddy, got out the mop and scrubbed away at the floors. It has been said that peasants, free to enter this luxurious temple of the rich for the first time, brought pigs into the lobby.

Mobs stormed casinos to vandalize the slot machines that had been unacknowledged fountains of bribe money

MORE THAN ONE MILLION PEOPLE JAMMED THE PLAZA AROUND THE PRESIDENTIAL PALACE TO HEAR FIDEL CASTRO SPEAK ABOUT THE NEW REVOLUTION ON JANUARY 21, 1959. NOTICE THAT NONE OF THE SIGNS MENTION SOCIALISM OR COMMUNISM. CASTRO HAD NOT YET ALIGNED HIMSELF WITH THE SOVIET UNION.

for the Batista family. One classic Hollywood moment came when the movie star George Raft defended the casino he had a stake in by standing on the front steps and daring the mob to try to enter. The crowd backed off, but the casinos were living on borrowed time once Batista had left. Cuba was about to change dramatically. Castro, after all, had already said, "We are ready to not only deport the gangsters, but to shoot them too."

THE NEW CUBA

On January 2, Castro gave a victory speech in Santiago de Cuba, wherein he promised the country that his revolution would not end like the one in 1898, when the United States had come in and run things. Castro began a victory drive from Santiago to Havana, where he was met by tens of thousands of cheering people. White doves were released from a cage as Castro spoke in central Havana. As though choreographed, one of the doves flew up into the sky and then came down and perched on Fidel's shoulder. This event held incredible symbolic power for many Cubans, and caused a collective gasp. (In *Santería,* the African-derived faith common in Cuba, doves are associated with Obatalá, an important *orisha,* or deity. That the dove landed on Fidel was a sign to the faithful that he had been chosen by the gods.) The Revolution, as Cubans now call the years under Fidel, had begun. Soon after taking power, Castro put the policeman who had saved his life after the attack on the Moncada barracks in charge of his personal security.

People all over the world applauded Castro's victory, because the revolution was seen as a truly popular revolt and its leader was a charismatic man. In New York and in Miami Cubans cheered the fall of Batista. Even the U.S. government was guardedly optimistic (Castro had yet to proclaim himself a Marxist-Leninist).

The United States and Cuba had a decent relationship for the first months of the revolution—in April Castro even visited New York, where he made several speeches and was received as a hero—but the good public relations did not last long.

By the spring Castro had executed hundreds of political opponents and tightened his grip on the country. One of Castro's first moves was to order the U.S. military advisers to leave the country, because they had helped train Batista's soldiers. The United States became even less pleased as the first few months passed and Castro took possession of various U.S. companies, including the huge oil refineries, in the name of Cuba. In October 1960, he nationalized 165 United States–owned businesses, including Kodak, Westinghouse, Woolworth, Canada Dry, and Goodyear. He began to make friendly gestures toward the Soviet Union (which hadn't provided any support for the revolution), and that country began sending Castro weapons. On January 3, 1961, after Castro kicked eleven U.S. diplomats out of the country, the United States and Cuba broke diplomatic relations.

It was not until after this break that Castro declared himself to be a Marxist-Leninist, and Cuba a socialist country. In the middle of the Cold War this declaration was considered to be an unveiled challenge to the United States. For the Cubans and for Castro (who as recently as 1958 had spoken derisively of the Communist Party in Cuba), the declaration of a socialist state might have been driven more by economic necessity and the hope that the Russians would help the island than by any ideological imperatives. Either way, it was a decisive and incredibly divisive move that led to an ill-fated invasion.

That spring, CIA-trained Cuban exiles hit the beach at Playa Girón, or the Bay of Pigs, and were easily overcome. In retrospect it is hard to imagine what was going through the heads of the CIA chiefs who thought their fifteen hundred men would be able to succeed against a revolutionary army of sixty thousand. In fact, in the days following this small invasion, about which the Cubans had received warning in advance from spies, Castro waited for what he thought was going to be the "real" invasion, the arrival of U.S. Marines. The attack never materialized, but all hope of good relations between the two countries was lost. Over the next three decades, which included the Cuban Missile Crisis, U.S. attempts to kill Castro with exploding cigars, still more attempts at invading Cuba, and the Cuban training and arming of revolutionary movements in Central America, the two countries moved further and further apart. To the detriment of the economic and cultural life of both nations, Cuba and the United States have been unable to come to terms with one another.

THE REVOLUTION CHANGED CUBAN SOCIETY FROM TOP TO BOTTOM. ONE OF THE MORE REMARKABLE DIFFERENCES
WAS THE COMPLETE DISAPPEARANCE OF CONSUMER ADVERTISING. BILLBOARDS AND NOTICES
FOR LAUNDRY SOAPS, SOFT DRINKS, AND CARS WERE REPLACED BY ANOTHER KIND OF PROPAGANDA.

☰ A REVOLUTION IN RETROSPECT

Castro's revolution inspired intense reactions on all sides. People seem to see it as either the greatest social achievement in the history of the Americas or as a traitorous attack on civilization. When the more than thirty-five years of revolution are looked at calmly and rationally, it can be seen as a mixture of both. Castro is not the angel that many would-be fifth columnists paint him to be, but neither is he the wicked oppressor portrayed by Washington.

From the beginning, Castro has treated the Cuban people as his children, to be protected and raised—as long as they obey their father. He took over a country that had aching poverty alongside incredible riches at a time when about one fourth of the adults could not read or write and about one fourth of all men were unable to find work, and evened things out a bit (or destroyed everything, depending on your point of view). Castro was able to take power in the first place because many Cubans were totally dissatisfied with the Batista government, especially with the corruption and crime that accompanied Batista's dealings. At first Cubans in general welcomed Castro, if guardedly, but his attack on the class system was too much for some people to take.

One of his most significant first actions was to break up the huge planta-

tions and turn the land over to the peasants who had worked it. Of course, these actions enraged the wealthy Cubans and Americans who had businesses on the island. Many of these Cubans fled Castro's program of nationalization, establishing exile communities in Florida, Puerto Rico, and Mexico. From these spots the expatriates could freely criticize the government and even launch assaults on the country. The heads of North American businesses that held interests in Cuba let their irritation be known to the U.S. government.

IMPERIALIST OUTPOST

The only place you can get a Big Mac in Cuba is on Guantánamo Naval Base, a fenced-off parcel of land that has been occupied by the U.S. military since 1898. Not many Cubans pass through these golden arches.

For the first half of the twentieth century the local economy depended on Gitmo (as the sailors call the base) for jobs. The sailors in turn relied on the town of Caimanera for bars, women, and entertainment. But after Castro's revolution the gates between Cuba and Gitmo were permanently closed. Except for a few aging Cubans who've always worked for Uncle Sam, no one is allowed to enter or leave the forty-five-square-mile (38.8 sq. km) base from Cuban soil.

The U.S. troops have orders to shoot to kill any Cuban soldiers who approach the base, although more than one U.S. Navy sailor has bought rum, cigars, and even marijuana through the fence from the locals. Other cultural exchanges take place via television: sets on the Cuban side of the base are privileged to pick up the same *Gilligan's Island* reruns that the U.S. soldiers watch, and the North Americans are able to watch Castro's long speeches exhorting patriotism and sacrifice on national holidays.

Cubans wanting to flee the country sometimes swim or boat through the shark-infested bay to reach the base, and sometimes die trying. Others have made it by land. Whoever arrives is spirited to the United States and given refugee status.

The base is a thorn in Castro's side, a painful reminder of how the United States dominates Cuba to this day. The leased agreement for the land was adopted into the original Cuban constitution, and will expire only when both sides agree it should. So far the United States has not capitulated. Castro never cashes the $4,085 rent check he receives each year from the U.S. Navy.

PAPER DOVES DECORATE A STREET IN EASTERN CUBA IN PREPARATION FOR A FESTIVAL (PREVIOUS PAGES). THE DOVES ARE ASSOCIATED WITH THE SANTERIA DEITY CALLED OBATALA, AND ALSO RECALL THE DOVES THAT LANDED ON CASTRO'S SHOULDER DURING HIS VICTORY SPEECH IN HAVANA AT THE END OF THE REVOLUTION.

MIAMI'S OLDER CUBAN EXILES DREAM OF RETURNING TO THE CLEAN, QUIET CUBA OF THEIR YOUTH (ABOVE), WHERE THEY CAN SIT AND ENJOY THE WORLD THEY LEFT BEHIND. BUT THE CUBA THEY REMEMBER HAS LARGELY DISAPPEARED.

Previous pages: © Marc Pokempner This page: © Nancy Stout

The exodus grew over time. Within a year of his assumption of power Castro was making many Cubans, especially those with money and education, nervous. Fearing that Castro would soon make it illegal to leave the country, many of these dissatisfied Cubans fled for Miami in any way they could. Like most immigrants, these Cubans arrived with no idea of what they would do once in the United States. Miami at the time was a small town with a small Cuban population. It was soon to become a cultural and financial headquarters for all of Latin America, centered around the Cuban exile community.

The first Cuban exiles were a mixed bag of poor and wealthy, educated and uneducated, and they were welcomed with open arms by a country that hated communism. While it is widely believed that Cubans have been so successful in the United States because they arrived with bags of money, boxes full of diplomas, and address books full of good connections, many of them arrived with little more than the clothes on their backs and a few dollars in their pockets.

Relief organizations helped them relocate around the country or find housing and work in Miami. Little by little they established a strong community. These days Miami is home to Latin Americans from many countries, and the Cubans have largely left their first neighborhood, which was centered around Calle Ocho (Eighth Street), near downtown. In the long tradition of immigration to the United States, these Cubans have earned a little money and moved to the suburbs—even those who arrived in the *Mariel* boatlift in the early 1980s have by now assimilated. For the most part, however, Cubans in North America do not consider themselves immigrants. Despite their success on foreign soil, they are *en exilio*, waiting for the day they can return to Cuba. Some of the noisier Cubans in Miami insist that they want to rule Cuba again. But many more just want to go back to the country they love, build a little house with a front porch, and sit and watch the day go by in what has always been called "the ever-faithful isle."

CROWDS THRONGED THE PLAZAS OF HAVANA IN CELEBRATION OF THE 1958 REVOLUTION, BUT IN A FEW YEARS MANY PEOPLE WERE FLEEING CASTRO'S CUBA.

Archive Photos

CHAPTER four

PASSIONS

WELL-PRESERVED U.S. AUTOMOBILES IN CUBA ARE TIME CAPSULES THAT TESTIFY TO THE STRONG TIES THAT EXIST BETWEEN THE TWO COUNTRIES, DESPITE THE POLITICAL RAVAGES OF THE COLD WAR.

Cubans are truly a mixed breed, born of the collision of many cultures, including French, Chinese, and North American, although the primary blood of Cuba is West African and Spanish. This blood, with its inherent contradictions, is at the heart of the rich traditions that define the country.

About one third of Cubans are considered black. Most are descendants of slaves brought from what are now Senegal, Gambia, Guinea, the Congo, and Nigeria (some even continue to pass on the Yoruba language to their children, especially for religious ceremonies). Others migrated from Haiti, the Bahamas, and other islands in the Caribbean, where their ancestors, too, were slaves. And African blood runs through almost everyone else in Cuba, whether or not they choose to acknowledge it. Although many people are light-skinned and light-eyed, there are very few Cuban-born pure-blood Spanish people left on the island. As the saying goes, *El que no tiene de Congo, tiene de Carabanei:* "If your ancestors weren't from the Congo they must have been from Carabanei (a region in southwestern Senegal)."

A few Chinese remain on the island, descendants of indentured servants brought over to build railroads and work the plantations in the nineteenth century. Most people of Chinese descent have since left the country, leaving Havana's Chinatown quite desolate. The city has tried to restore life into this small neighborhood by building Chinese-style arches over some streets and small pedestrian malls, but the most telling details of the culture that once filled this now-desolate barrio are the faded signs offering chop suey that are left over from the days before Fidel's revolution. The rest of the country's ten million people are primarily whites and criollos, the latter of whom are living testimony to the country's turbulent past.

Africans were at the bottom of society when they arrived as slaves; unfortunately, racism continued to play a big role in Cuba after the end of slavery.

THESE BOYS (OPPOSITE, TOP) ARE PLAYING WITH A PUPPY ON THE WIDE TERRACE THAT FACES EL MORRO IN HAVANA.
THE SCHOOLCHILDREN (ABOVE AND OPPOSITE, BOTTOM) SHOW THE VARIETY OF ETHNIC INFLUENCES ON THE PEOPLE
OF CUBA. FREE EDUCATION BECAME WIDELY AVAILABLE AFTER THE CUBAN REVOLUTION, AND THERE ARE CHILDREN IN SCHOOL
UNIFORMS EVERYWHERE ON THE ISLAND.

DRAMATIC COLORS POP OUT AT EVERY TURN IN CUBA, AS EVIDENCED BY THIS SCENE OF A WOMAN STANDING ON THE BALCONY OF HER DECAYING BUILDING (OPPOSITE PAGE), AND THIS YOUNG BOY LEAPING OFF THE MALECON IN HAVANA INTO THE CRASHING SEA.

Racism in Cuba is peculiar. Though Cuba has had its years of intense racial segregation, ever since the days of slavery there has been a great cultural integration in the country, and many of Cuba's heroes, such as Antonio Maceo, have been black. An extreme example of this dichotomy is that President Batista, who was of mixed blood, would not have been allowed to join the Havana Yacht Club, which was for whites only. Since the 1958 revolution there has been an effort to wipe out racism, and blacks have made many gains, but one look at the ruling congress will tell you that light-skinned Cubans still make the rules.

Yet Cuba now officially considers itself to be an Afro-Cuban country, and the beautiful beaches are filled with all shades of skin color, from the brightest burnt red to the deepest ebony, barely

A YOUNG STUDENT READS TO HER PRIMARY SCHOOL CLASS.

North Wind Picture Archive

MANY CHINESE WERE BROUGHT IN TO CUBA AS INDENTURED SERVANTS IN THE NINETEENTH CENTURY TO WORK THE PLANTATIONS AND SUGAR MILLS. ONCE-FLOURISHING CHINATOWNS IN HAVANA AND ELSEWHERE LARGELY DISAPPEARED AS CUBAN-CHINESE FLED THE ISLAND FOLLOWING THE 1958 REVOLUTION.

of themselves as citizens of the country they inhabit, but rather remain refugees from the country they love. On the island itself one of the highest compliments you could pay someone would be to say they are 100 percent *Cubano*.

≋ BEISBOL

Surprisingly, for a country that has spent the better part of one hundred years trying to distance itself from North American influence, baseball could be considered a 100 percent Cuban activity. One theorist has even gone so far as to posit that the game did not originate in the United States, but actually grew out of a game the Taíno Indians played called *batey*. Wherever it originated, baseball has been wildly popular since the mid-nineteenth century, and now every town in Cuba has a team and a stadium.

While the Cuban government prohibits players from joining professional teams off the island, Cubans are widely thought to be the best amateur players in the world. They have won over 80 percent of world championships in the last quarter century, and scouts from the National and American leagues in the United States regularly pay visits to the island to see who looks promising.

Cuban baseball has remained more a game than a business or profession, and all the accolades in the world don't change the fact that baseball is an egali-

covered with *tangas* (tiny bathing suits) and *tanguitas* (really tiny bathing suits). Segregation among Cubans is prohibited by law. Perhaps because of the centuries of struggle they faced to liberate themselves from Spain, and the many battles they have fought in the twentieth century, Cubans of all races are intensely nationalistic. Even when Cubans are away from the island, they often do not think

BASELINE IS A SERIOUS SUBJECT FOR THE PLAYER FROM HOLGUIN (RIGHT), AND FOR THE STICKBALL PLAYER (BELOW, RIGHT) WHO NO DOUBT IMAGINES THAT HIS SWING WILL KNOCK THE BALL OUT OF THE STADIUM, OR AT LEAST TO THE END OF THE PLAZA. THIS GENTLEMAN (OPPOSITE PAGE) PICKED AN UNIMPORTANT GAME TO ATTEND AT HAVANA STADIUM.

tarian sport that permeates the country from top to bottom. The streets of Habana Vieja are imaginary stadiums for kids with bats made from broomsticks swinging at tennis balls, which bounce off the eighteenth-century stone walls and the hoods of old American cars. Wiry grandfathers who can no longer throw a decent pitch gather every day under the catalpa trees in Central Park in Havana to talk baseball. Baseball is more than a sport in Cuba—it is one of life's necessities.

≋ THE SACRED AND THE PROFANE

While it is debatable whether or not baseball originated in Cuba, two aspects of Cuban culture that are indisputably *Cubano* are the religion called Santería and the rich mix of African rhythms and European instrumentation that is the backbone of Cuban music. The two go hand-in-hand, one influencing the other,

© Marc PoKempner

© Marc PoKempner

both with strong roots in the African past. The mix of religion and music might seem sacrilegious to tradition-bound Christians, but Cuban culture allows for a sense of celebration in its religion that is marvelous. At the same time, Cuban music adopts some aspects of the sacred side of life.

On a typical evening in modern Havana you might finish your meager meal of rice and perhaps some beans and eggs (if you're lucky and your ration card allows it) and then meet your friends who are killing time along the Malecón waiting for something to happen and watching the tide. After tracking down some cigarettes and maybe a bottle or two of Havana Club rum, you pile onto Chinese Flying Pigeon bikes (two people to each) and ride across the dark streets of Havana to someone's small house for a party.

One of you bends down to the Santería altar set up in the corner, lights an old stogey, and blows smoke over the saint to fill him up and make him happy before the party begins. Because the saint wants a drink, you take a mouthful of rum and spray it in a fine mist over

---

HAVANA STADIUM FIGURES PROMINENTLY IN THE SOCIAL LIFE OF MANY CUBANS, ALTHOUGH SOME GAMES JUST AREN'T GOOD ENOUGH TO DRAW THE CROWDS.

© Ernesto Bazan

the plaster figure. Finally, you set the cigar, burning, on top of a small glass of rum and leave it there, assured that the party will go well, with everyone smoking and drinking and dancing to hypnotic *rumba* music punctuated with beats from the sacred *tambor bata*.

This mix of the sacred and the profane permeates Cuban life (seeking the blessing of a saint before a party is just one minor aspect of Cuban religious practices). These days about one in every hundred Cubans is a practicing Christian, which in Cuban terms usually

THE MALECON IS THE CENTRAL MEETING SPOT OF HAVANA, WHERE YOU'LL SEE EVERYTHING FROM WOMEN PERFORMING SANTERIA RITUALS TO RASTAFARIANS TRYING TO SCORE MARIJUANA.

means Catholic. The Catholic church is still working out a relationship with the Castro government after more than thirty years of being discouraged, but in the last few years Catholicism has become

more accepted. Nonetheless, many of those who call themselves Catholics also believe in Santería (or in other, more mysterious religions of African descent). This animistic religion developed out of beliefs that came to the Caribbean and Brazil with the Yoruban slaves from West Africa. Called *Lucumí* in Cuba, this early religion was greatly influenced by Spanish Catholicism, and the early practitioners adopted the names of Christian saints for their traditional saints as a way of honoring what they respected in Christianity and of appeasing the

© Marc PoKempner

This photo: © Richard Riddell Opposite page: © Marc PoKempner

IN TERMS OF U.S. AUTOMOBILES, TIME STOPPED WHEN CASTRO TOOK POWER. THE ONLY NEW MODELS FROM DETROIT ARE DRIVEN BY FOREIGN DIPLOMATS, AND PARTS ARE HARD TO FIND. MOST AUTOMOBILES IN CUBA THESE DAYS ARE STYLELESS RUSSIAN MACHINES, BUT IN A TRIBUTE BOTH TO THE MANUFACTURING METHODS OF 1940S AND 50S DETROIT, AND TO CUBAN INGENUITY, OLD U.S. CARS ARE STILL SEEN EVERYWHERE ON THE ISLAND, THEIR SCRATCHES TOUCHED UP WITH HOUSEPAINT, THEIR CARBU-RETORS HELD TOGETHER WITH HOME-MADE NUTS AND BOLTS, AND THEIR LARGE ENGINES GUZZLING PRECIOUS GAS AT AN ASTONISHING RATE.

© Marc PoKempner

DANCE IS AN INTEGRAL PART OF CUBAN LIFE. HERE MEN AND WOMEN IN TRADITIONAL COSTUMES PERFORM DANCES PASSED DOWN THROUGH THE GENERATIONS. THE AFRICAN INFLUENCE IN CLOTHING AND MOVEMENT IS STRONG.

Spanish, who saw Lucumí as pagan. The blend of faiths became known as Santería, which means, literally, "saint worship." A basic belief is that destiny is determined before birth in *Ilé-Olofi*, or "God's house." Santería is appealing to many people because it doesn't have the arbitrary moral proscriptions that Catholicism does. Santería revels in the sensuous. The orishas like to have a good time.

SANTERIA

It is not unusual to enter a Catholic church in Cuba and see shrines to saints that you wouldn't see in Rome, and to see parishioners in trancelike states or reciting exotic prayers and incantations. Small ferries cross Havana harbor frequently for the little town of Regla. Most of the passengers are commuters coming from and going to work, but many are crossing to worship at the church and Santería shrine that rest side by side on the harbor's edge. Even those Catholics who don't actively follow Santería practices will stop at the shrine to pay their respects to the saint called Yemayá and say a prayer. The simple church is always filled with devout Habaneros and others from all ends of the country.

Followers of Santería believe that there is a celestial empire ruled over by Olofi, who is so supreme that humans could not hope to communicate directly with him. Under Olofi are the revered corps of Santería, the orishas. These saints (there are over four hundred) have human qualities and needs and act as intermediaries between humans and Olofi. The primary purpose of *santeros*, or "priests," is to honor the saints, obey them, interpret their commands for the faithful, and perform the rituals they demand. For this devotion, the santeros are given supernatural abilities to see into the future and shape it, and are protected against evil. It is not a religion of proselytizers. In fact, it is a very private, mysterious faith, the power of which rests in its magical nature.

DANCERS RECREATE A CARNAVAL DANCE IN AN ELABORATE COURTYARD AT A FESTIVAL IN SANTIAGO DE CUBA. THE COSTUMES SHOW A DRAMATIC MIX OF AFRICAN AND SPANISH STYLES.

THESE MUSICIANS (OPPOSITE PAGE) PAUSE IN THE COURTYARD OF A TRINIDAD RESTAURANT TO LISTEN AS THEIR LEADER GOES OVER SOME COMPLICATED RHYTHMS. THEY'LL PERFORM FOR TOURISTS LATER IN THE AFTERNOON, AND THEN CUT AWAY TO THE CASA DE LA TROVA TO PLAY INTO THE NIGHT. CELEBRANTS (RIGHT, TOP AND BOTTOM) PERFORM TRADITIONAL MUSIC AND DANCE AT THE CARIFEST IN THE MAIN SQUARE OF SANTIAGO DE CUBA.

© Marc PoKempner

This photo: © Marc PoKempner Opposite page: © Stephen Williams

"LONG LIVE CHANGO"

BY CELINA GONZALEZ AND REUTILIO DOMINGUEZ

"Santa Bárbara (Que Viva Changó!)," a song by the great Cuban singer Celina González, is an emotional celebration of faith that honors both the Catholic saint Bárbara and the Santería deity Changó. With the release of this song in 1948 González and her husband Reutilio Domínguez became the first popular musicians to sing about Santería, and the song took Cuba by storm. It has probably been recorded more than any other Cuban song, and there aren't too many Cubans who don't know the lyrics.

Long live Changó
Long live Changó
Long live Changó
Long live Changó, everyone

Blessed Santa Bárbara
My poetry pours out for you
and is inspired by emotion
before your beautiful image

With infinite will
I pull from my heart
this melody
asking that from heaven
You send us comfort
and your blessed benediction
Venerated and pure virgin
blessed Santa Bárbara
Our favorite prayer
we are lifting up to you

With happiness and tenderness
I want to lift up my ballad
to your sacred mansion
where goodness shines
together with your divine cup
and your saintly sword

In the name of my country
Santa Bárbara I ask
that you water us with
your sacred blessing

From my heart I too
send you my prayers
with pride and power
It will be that your name rises

In the name of my Cuba
I send you this salute

In Santería, each follower learns who his or her patron saint is from the santero in a series of ceremonies that initiate a person into the faith. Some of the principal orishas, along with their colors, influences, and corresponding Catholic saints (a male orisha might have a female saint's name), appear below.

≋ ≋ ≋

Obatalá, who wears white and gold, was the first orisha created by Olofi. He is also known as Our Lady of Mercy, and is associated with purity and peace.

Ellegua, who wears black and red, and is also known as Saint Anthony, is the messenger of the orishas. Without him nothing can happen. He once used *ewe*, or healing herbs, to cure Olofi when he was sick. Ellegua guards the gates of Christian purgatory.

Changó, who wears red, and is also known as Saint Barbara, is aligned with lightning and dance and is a great warrior.

Yemayá, who wears blue, is also known as Our Lady of Regla, patron saint of the ports of Havana and Matanzas. She is the mother of fourteen of the most powerful orishas.

Babalú-Ayé, also called Saint Lazarus, who wears purple, is lord of health and epidemics.

Oshún, who wears yellow, is represented by Our Lady of Charity, the patron saint of Cuba. (The most famous church in Cuba, El Cobre, outside of Santiago de Cuba, honors this saint.) Almost all Cubans, whether they follow Santería, Catholicism, or both, revere Our Lady of Charity. Los exilios have an impressive chapel honoring her in Miami.

≋ ≋ ≋

The saints are worshiped in a variety of secretive and complex rituals that include chanting, animal sacrifice, dancing, and music. Some rituals are more serious than others. Devout Catholics who don't really follow Santería might light candles for a deity like Our Lady of Charity. Devout followers of Santería might go further into rituals, which are often derisively and incorrectly called black magic or voodoo by outsiders, such as slitting a chicken's throat and draining the blood into a chalice. Walking through cemeteries in Cuba it is not uncommon to come across a small black doll that has been used in a Santería ritual. Or you might be walking through a park or forest and see a doll resting in the crook of a tree. The religion permeates Cuban society. There probably isn't a person in Cuba who doesn't know at least part of the lyrics to the popular devotional song "Que Viva Changó!," by Celina González. And everyone loves Carnaval.

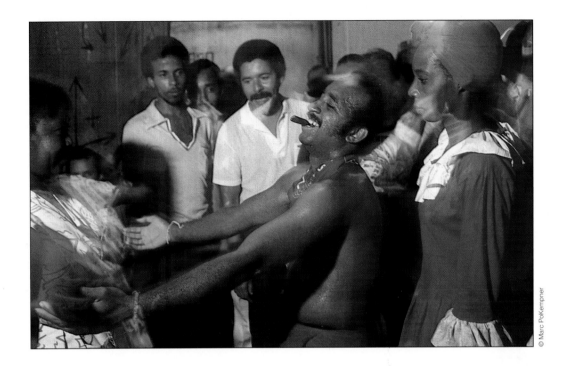

THE RELIGIOUS RITUALS OF SANTERIA ARE OFTEN CELEBRATORY, AND SOMETIMES THE DEVOTEES, SUCH AS THE MAN PICTURED HERE, FALL INTO TRANCES.

≋ CARNAVAL

Carnaval in Cuba, as in parts of Brazil, is a grand expression of African and Catholic traditions that grew out of the Yoruban practice of singing praise to the saints. Each saint in the Yoruban pantheon has a specific rhythm and dance, and under Spanish rule the slaves molded their festival to fit the Day of Kings. The slaves would parade past reviewing stands so that their masters could watch the festivities. The dancing groups were called *camparsas* and had drummers, singers, and trumpeters. Much of Cuban music grew out of Carnaval and other celebrations. Rumba, mambo, and conga rhythms can be traced to the ritual music of the *Palo Monte* sect of Lucumí that was founded by slaves brought from the Congo.

For five days in late July the city of Santiago de Cuba is the frenzied center of Carnaval in Cuba. The streets of this steaming coastal city are taken over by camparsas and other groups. Each day the main procession leads off with people dressed in traditional costumes from the slave days: the women wear long skirts and colored blouses and the men wear tight shirts, wide belts, and medium-length trousers. They are followed by camparsas dancing and gyrating to singers, musicians playing long whiny Chinese trumpets, and an impossible number of drums, some of which symbolize the ancestors talking. Congas are

danced, with people leaping hypnotically in and out of the lines. Spectators will join in at one block and drift away a few blocks later. The streets and balconies are festooned with lights and colored paper, and there is beer and rum to be had at every turn. Coming after the

sugar harvest, this celebration offers a tremendous release to the city. Each day is a little wilder than the day before. At the end of the day the rumba music takes over and people dance all night, every night, until the final evening of intense celebration.

≋ MUSIC

While religion and music mix perfectly in the celebratory heart of Cuban culture, you don't need to believe in God to experience the magic of Cuban music. This small island has had as much influence on twentieth-century popular music and jazz as almost any other country in the world. The Taíno, the Spanish, and the African slaves all had their own forms of music, but perhaps the first truly distinctive Cuban music was the Colonial *contradanza*, a formal dance music that was heavily influenced by French music of the seventeenth century. This music developed into the *danzón* style, and these stiff rhythms are still popular in Cuba, especially on Saturday night in the central park of Matanzas.

The ornately arpeggiated piano style propelled by a 2/4 beat that is danzón seems to have been a bit of a formal deviation in the development of Cuban music. The true soul of Cuban music would have to be *guajira,* or country music. It is speculated that the African drums and Spanish guitars of guajira probably first met in seventeenth-century Havana bohios, where freed slaves served sailors food and drink and played music for them. Guajira music really exploded in the eastern provinces called Guantánamo and Oriente. Myriad rhythms and arrangements have tumbled out of guajira in a never-ending number of musical styles, including *criolla,* rumba,

IN THE OLD PHOTOGRAPH ON THE OPPOSITE PAGE, COSTUMED CUBAN DANCERS FULFILL THE ROMANTIC EXPECTATIONS TOURISTS HAVE OF THE ISLAND. THIS BAND PERFORMING FOR A CROWD IN FRONT OF HAVANA'S CATHEDRAL MUST HAVE JUST BEGUN, BECAUSE NO ONE SEEMS TO BE DANCING YET.

son, son montuno, son changüi, bolero, trova, conga, mambo, *cha cha chá* (which, for some reason, is abbreviated to cha cha in the United States), *tango, charanga,* Cuban jazz, *guaguancóin, pachanga, nueva trova, songo,* and *salsa.* (Many Cuban musicians say that salsa, which has Colombian and Puerto Rican influences, is not Cuban music. Salsa, which means "sauce" in Spanish, is something these musicians keep on their tables to spice up plates of *picadillo,* not something they play)

"Guantanamera" is a classic example of guajira music, and is without a doubt the most famous Cuban song ever recorded, with versions by everyone from Julio Iglesias (breathy and romantic, with lots of strings) to Pete Seeger (very poorly pronounced and translated). The original lyrics were by Joseito Fernandez, based on Martí's writing, but almost every Cuban has developed his own lyrics. This is painfully evident late at night in bars when the audience is invited to sing along to a version of the song. Cubans never seem to tire of this tune.

⟨≋⟩ RUMBA, SON, AND ON AND ON

Despite the popularity of "Guantanamera," rumba and its offspring son have had much more direct influence on modern Cuban music than guajira. Almost all Cuban music and dance reflects one of the three types of rumba: *yambu*, the oldest, slowest, and most sensual rumba, played by groups like Los Muñequitos de Matanzas, with the rhythm often coming from a wooden box called a *cajón; guaguanco*, which is faster; and *colombia*, which is fast and intensely polyrhythmic, with dialogues between the drummers (sometimes the drummers will even try to anticipate with their rhythms the moves the dancers are going to make). Watching traditional rumba dancers act out their small plays of love, betrayal, violence, and sex is a vividly memorable experience.

Son and its various permutations are all founded on the the basic syncopated one-two/one-two-three (or the reverse) rhythm played on *claves* (heavy wooden sticks) that is the backbone of Cuban music. There is usually a repeated chorus in the middle or at the end of the

© Stephen Williams

THESE DANCERS (ABOVE) ARE MOVING TO THE TUNES OF PANAMANIAN "DANCE HALL" RAPPER EL GENERAL AFTER SCHOOL IN THE EASTERN TOWN OF BARACOA. CELIA CRUZ (OPPOSITE PAGE) PERFORMS.

© David Redfern/Retna Ltd.

song, and the rest of the vocals are often improvised. Old son music often depended on an unusual nasal vocal style known as *voz de vieja*, or "old woman's voice." The deepest roots of salsa music reach into changüi, a very old version of son, from Guantánamo. It started around the turn of the century when West African rhythms were combined with the *tres* (small guitar with three sets of double strings) from Spain. Son was first thought to be primitive and overtly sexual—immoral, in other words. As with most immoral music, however, son was too infectious to contain. Son spread across Cuba and up to the United States in the 1920s, and even went around the world to influence music in West Africa.

Changüi is fast son, and you dance to it with close steps. A modern group called Orquesta Revé reproduces the voz de vieja, and its leader, Elio Revé, has done much to keep the music very popular. Revé was a founding member of the wildly popular group Los Van Van. His newer group, Orquesta Revé, has no drum set, but uses the tambor bata from Santería music, claves, bongos, maracas, bells, and congas.

≋ THE MUSICAL PANTHEON

Revé is only one of the many influential musicians Cuba has produced over the years. Other famous musicians and groups of the twentieth century are listed below.

Celia Cruz was the premier salsa vocalist, whose passionate recording of "Bemba Colora" is a classic. An exile who has charted the development of salsa music from its infancy, she has recorded countless records and is an indefatigable promoter of the form.

Pedro Luis Ferrer is a contemporary singer in the long tradition of Cuban protest music. A hero to many young people in Cuba, Ferrer has been imprisoned for his songs. A cassette recording of a song wherein he refers to Castro as a bullying, out-of-touch grandfather is widely circulated in Cuba, though listening to it is strictly forbidden.

Enrique Jorrin is the father of cha cha chá. This is an onomatopoeic name, because "cha cha chá" imitates the sound made by the *guiro* player. The music has a light midtempo beat that doesn't even hint at the passions of other Cuban rhythms, and spawned a popular dance style in the 1950s.

Ernesto Leucona is the composer of the haunting song "Siboney," which Bing Crosby crooned to the music of bandleader Xavier Cugat and his orchestra. Known as the King of the Rumba, Cugat was the driving force behind the rumba dance craze that took hold in the United States in the 1930s.

Machito, a bandleader, singer, and maraca player whose real name was Frank Raul Grillo, was considered very hip in New York in the 1950s and played with Dizzy Gillespie and Charlie Parker during one of the most creative periods for jazz and Latin music.

Benny Moré was called *El Bárbaro del Ritmo*, or "The Rhythm Barbarian." His records show off his remarkable voice and gift for son montuno and Cuban jazz in general.

Isaac Oviedo, now almost ninety years old, is a master of the tres guitar, which is at the center of son montuno. In the 1940s and 1950s, son montuno spread throughout the Caribbean and United

© David Redfern/Retna Ltd

© Marc PoKempner

CHUCHO VALDÉZ (LEFT) IS
THE LEADER OF THE VERY POPULAR
GROUP IRAKERE. LOCAL MUSICIANS
(BELOW, LEFT) PERFORM PURELY
FOR PLEASURE AT THE
CASA DE LA TROVA IN TRINIDAD.
SILVIO RODRIGUEZ (OPPOSITE, TOP).
MACHITO (OPPOSITE, BOTTOM).

States and influenced the big band
sound. Oviedo revolutionized tres playing in the 1920s and 1930s and is considered a great vocalist. Due to its African
influences, the style he devised, called
Afroson, has many similarities to North
American blues music.

Chano Pozo wrote "Manteca," one of the
most famous Afro-Cuban jazz songs.
This was a giant hit for Dizzy Gillespie's
Big Band in the 1940s.

Perez Prado, an incredibly talented
pianist, is widely considered the master-
mind behind the mambo style. In fact,
he was known as the Mambo King.

Arsenio Rodríguez has almost been
forgotten, but in 1936 he wrote one of
the first mambos, a mix of Cuban and
African rhythms and contrapuntal horns.
Always aware of his roots, Rodríguez
wrote lyrics that celebrated the African
experience in Cuba. He said his music
had *ritmo diablo*, "devil's rhythm," and felt

© Marc PoKempner

© David Redfern/Retna Ltd.

it could send people into a trance. He moved to the United States late in life, looking for a cure for his encroaching blindness, and died in poverty in Los Angeles, an unknown musician in a strange land.

Silvio Rodríguez and *Pablo Milanés* are two musicians who have come of age since the 1958 revolution. Their style, called nueva trova, or "new ballad," adds revolutionary fervor and social commentary to the traditional love-and-loss lyrics of trova.

Gonzalo Roig founded the Havana Symphony Orchestra and in 1932 adapted the Cuban writer Cirilo Villaverder's novel *Cecial Valdéz*, about love between a mixed-blood woman and a Spanish acristocrat, for the opera, using rumba, guaracha, conga, contradanza, and other Cuban styles. The libretto included many African idioms.

Chucho Valdéz is the leader of Irakere, which combines African-American music with Afro-Cuban rhythms in a distinctive jazz form.

Los Van Van is a group that plays a modern version of charanga, a turn-of-the-century musical style that uses flute, violins, piano, double bass, and various percussion instruments. They also play *songo*, which is a fairly new mix of son, rumba, and rock.

Zeus is an outcast heavy metal band that is based in Havana. Their music is fast and violent, and it's hard to find even a hint of son or rumba in the dark rhythms, but somehow the band's music sounds Cuban.

≋ THE PULSE OF LIFE

When a Cuban likes a performance, he might say it's *sabroso*, or "tasty," and it is easy to find delicious and filling music on the island. The streets of Habana Vieja are a cacophany of competing sounds from radios and stereos, and almost any bar or nightclub will have live musicians who are shockingly professional. Because music is such an integral part of the culture, there are countless unknowns who play their music out of pure joy and spiritual necessity on corners and in the wonderful *casas de la trova*, or "music halls," found in every Cuban town. Enter any casa de la trova, from a nondescript room in the countryside with peeling paint and nothing to drink to Santiago de Cuba's Casa de la Trova, with its photographs of famous musicians and a refrigerator full of rum and beer, and you will be welcomed into a special world where the pulse of Cuba will surround you. The rhythms of the past, and possibly the rhythms of the future, weave in and out of whatever music is being played. In Cuba, a revolutionary sound is always just a few beats of the clave away.

CHAPTER
five

BLUE SMOKE
AND RUM

WESTERN CUBA'S DRAMATIC AND BEAUTIFUL VUELTA ABAJO IS AN EXTRAORDINARILY FERTILE REGION OF THE COUNTRY.

Traveling west from Havana into the magnificent landscape of Pinar del Río province you'll come across a small roadside stand in the middle of nowhere built of bulging palm trunks, stalks of bamboo woven together with twine, and a thatched roof. Along with the expected palm nuts carved into masks and mass-produced florescent sunglasses, the people at this little bohio will sell you two of the most vital ingredients in the cultural and economic life of Cuba: sugar and tobacco.

A good way to try the sugar is in a *mojito*—a bracing mixture of rich Cuban rum, sugar, soda, and yerbabuena that has knocked the socks off tourists for many years. If you want an undiluted sugar infusion, order *guarapo,* and watch the barman whack a three-foot (1m)

length of fresh sugar cane with his machete and feed it into a machine that dispenses the viscous juice out one end and the fibrous pulp out the other. Drink up, because that's all there is to guarapo—sugar juice, pure and simple. That should satisfy your sweet tooth and give you a little charge to help you through the remainder of the day.

On the countertop you will see an array of the *tabacos* (cigars) and *cigarros* (cigarettes) that have made Cuba famous to smokers all over the world. Long, thick Cohibas, despite their simple labels, are among the finest and most expensive Cuban cigars. Delicious, fragrant, unfiltered H. Upmann cigarettes in their elegant yellow package are also treasured. Beware of these cigarros if you are used to filtered, light cigarettes, because H. Upmann's are the real thing, and they pack a wallop.

Sip your drink, blow your smoke rings, and enjoy the *organo* music coming over the radio. Your cares will seem far away as your tobacco and your sugar bring you into the heart of Cuba.

WHILE IN RECENT YEARS CUBA HAS TRIED TO MODERNIZE ITS ECONOMY WITH BIOTECHNOLOGY AND TOURISM, AGRICULTURE STILL REMAINS THE BEDROCK OF THE COUNTRY, AND THE RURAL AREAS STILL HAVE AN OLD-FASHIONED FEEL.

≋ SUGAR

There is an old Cuban saying that goes *Sin azúcar, no hay país*, which means, "Without sugar, there isn't a country." Although sugar is the backbone of Cuba, it is not native to the country. The cane is indigenous to New Guinea, and was cultivated in Asia for thousands of years before Columbus brought it to the Caribbean on his second voyage, in 1493. Cuba didn't have the strong, thin plants until Velázquez brought them in 1511. Once sugar cane arrived, however, it established itself with ease. It would be impossible to speak of Cuba today without mentioning sugar.

Before production began in the New World, sugar was a rare luxury in Europe. By the end of the sixteenth century it was starting to become common. The king of Spain authorized the building of sugar processing plants in 1595 and within a few years there were more than fifteen of them in operation, most supplied by Portuguese-run plantations. Demand continued to grow and by the end of the sixteenth century sugar production in the Caribbean was the largest business in the world.

Slavery was a big business, too. When the cane is ready for cutting there is no time to waste; the planters' need for free labor was therefore immense. West Africans were sold into slavery all over the Caribbean and flooded into Cuba to work the sugar plantations in

---

MOJITO

Ernest Hemingway no doubt quaffed a number of mojitos during his years in Havana, and La Bodeguita del Medio in Habana Vieja claims he favored their recipe. Here's how they make them.

1/2 teaspoon sugar
juice from 1/2 lime
two tablespoons
    yerbabuena (an herb
    found in Latin Ameri-
    can specialty stores)
    or fresh mint
ice
1 1/2 ounces light rum
soda water

Combine the sugar and the lime juice in a highball glass. Add the yerbabuena or mint and crush the leaves with a spoon to release the flavor. Add several ice cubes and the rum. Fill with soda and stir. Serve.

© Richard Riddell

MORNING MIST BEGINS TO
BURN OFF OF A FIELD IN THE
VUELTA ABAJO. THE MIX OF
HUMIDITY AND SUN COMBINE
TO MAKE THIS ONE OF THE
FINEST TOBACCO GROWING
REGIONS IN THE WORLD.

the coming years. Watched from high towers, they worked from dawn to dusk to satisfy the growing sweet tooth in Europe and the new American colonies. Harvesting the tall fibrous sugar cane was—and is—brutal and dangerous work. Hard fibers can scratch out an eye, and a careless cutter can easily whack off his foot instead of a stalk of cane with his sharp machete.

The sugar and slave trades really boomed in Cuba after the slave revolt in Haiti in 1791 caused most of the French sugar plantations to move to Cuba. Over the next few decades these plantations modernized the Cuban industry, introducing steam engines to run the rollers that squeezed the juice from the cane and, in the 1830s, railroads to haul the cane from the fields to the mills. After the cane was crushed the greenish guarapo was boiled down until it became thick, brown molasses, much thicker than what you would find for sale in a supermarket today. This molasses was purified, filtered, and refined even further until it could be molded into cones and loaves of moist, rough, brown sugar, which were easily transported. This type of sugar is still sold all over Latin America, and you can slice off a piece to sweeten drinks or food, or to eat as an energizing snack. Plantations that had the means to take the sugar from the field all the way to the mold were called *bateys*. By 1835 there were more than one thousand

© Marc PoKempner

mills processing over 198 million pounds (90 million kg) of sugar in Cuba, most of it for export.

In the nineteenth century the biggest plantations, called *ingenios,* resembled fiefdoms. There would be the ornate palace of the landowner; other nice houses for the manager, the administrator, the bookkeeper, the sugarmaster, and the machinist; and decent places for the workers who were paid salaries. On the early plantations the slaves lived in clusters of thatched bohios, but in later years they were kept in *barracones,* large buildings that had a series of oppressive, barred-in cells facing an inner courtyard. For the processing, there would be a barn for crushing the cane, another barn for boiling the molasses, and many outbuildings and sheds.

Between the late seventeenth century and the mid-nineteenth century the slave population jumped from about thirty thousand to almost half a million. Plantation owners financed slave traders and also paid to have Mexican Indians

A FIELD OF SUGAR CANE IN BLOOM (LEFT). **S**UGAR IS BY FAR THE MOST IMPORTANT CROP FOR **C**UBA, AND CITIZENS ARE SOMETIMES CALLED OFF THEIR REGULAR JOBS TO GO INTO THE FIELDS TO HELP WITH THE HARVEST.

WHILE MUCH OF THE HARVESTING IS NOW MECHANIZED, SOME WORKERS STILL USE OXEN AND CARTS TO HAUL CUT SUGARCANE OUT OF THE FIELDS, AND TO PLOW THE EARTH, JUST AS THEY DID IN THE EIGHTEENTH CENTURY. EVEN WITH MECHANIZATION, HOWEVER, HARVESTING SUGAR CANE IS LABOR INTENSIVE, DIRTY WORK. AND THE EQUIPMENT OFTEN BREAKS DOWN.

and Mongolians brought in as virtual slaves under a system of indentured servitude. Obviously the slaves were not willing workers, and the overlords enforced their rule with brute force, aided by dogs and whips. The slaves would sometimes work from well before dawn to well after dusk cutting the cane by hand and then transporting it on ox-drawn carts to the mill. The slaves had no time to grow food on the plots of land they were sometimes loaned and no time to rest or recover from the many tropical diseases that were common on the island. One in ten slaves died each year. What women there were were often abused and raped by the masters, and their children were put into slavery. It is said that sometimes groups of slaves would commit mass suicide in the hopes of finding a better life in the beyond rather than face the horrible conditions of the bateys.

At the end of the nineteenth century the Ten Years' War disrupted the entire sugar industry, leaving it wide open to change. North Americans rushed in with great sums of money and bought up plantations and bateys and modernized the industry. They developed systems for producing the highly purified, powdery white sugar the world loves today. The big sugar factories came to be known as *centrales* because they would process the cane for a lot of plantations over a wide area. By 1959 there were 161 factories in Cuba, and about half of them were owned by foreigners, mostly North Americans. At that time, one out of ten people in Cuba worked in the sugar industry. Sugar has remained central to the economy throughout the years of revolution.

Sugar is a type of grass that grows up to twenty feet (6.1m) high in the good Cuban soil, though it is rarely allowed to grow this tall before being

harvested. A plant will regenerate year after year for perhaps a decade. Then a piece of the top of the old cane is planted to start a new growth. The cane is cut between November and June, when it is about seven feet (2.1m) high and two inches (5cm) in diameter. Though much sugar harvesting is now done by machine, you will still have no trouble seeing men in the fields working from dawn to dusk. Working in lines, they move across a field, grabbing a stalk of cane with one hand and slashing it close to the ground with their stubby, wide machetes. They whack off the top of the plant, whack off the dried leaves, leave the stalk on the ground for another crew to pick up, and grab another plant. It is backbreaking work. Sometimes white egrets will follow the *macheteros* to peck at the bugs that are suddenly exposed to the world.

These days the cane is brought to the mills on carts or trucks or trains as quickly as possible to keep the juice in the canes from fermenting. Then it is crushed to release the guarapo, boiled with lime to purify it, and clarified to make it even more pure. Then it is cooked yet again to get rid of more of the moisture and left in evaporating pans until the sugar starts to crystallize. After the molasses is separated to make rum and cattle feed, sugar crystals are left. These brown crystals are raw sugar. Sometimes the sugar is processed further into white crystals for export, but

Previous, this, and opposite pages: © Marc PoKempner

most of the sugar processed in Cuba is left brown. The leftover plant fibers are sometimes burned to heat up boilers, or can even be used to make paper and building materials. Sugar cane is what keeps the country going.

🔰 TOBACCO

Although these days in Cuba, as elsewhere, smoking is gaining a bad reputation—even Fidel gave up his serious cigar habit in what he called a "heroic effort"—tobacco is ingrained in the Cuban culture. A common saying in Cuba is *Ella está infumable*, "she's unsmokable," which means that she is not looking very good. People smoke everywhere. You can board a train in

A GRAND CEIBA TREE (PREVIOUS PAGES). THIS INSECT-LIKE MACHINE (ABOVE) HAULS THE CUT CANE FROM THE GROUND AND DROPS IT IN WAGONS TO BE HAULED TO THE REFINERY. A MAN SMOKES THE FRUITS OF HIS LABOR AS HE WORKS (BELOW).

© Richard Riddell

Santiago de Cuba and end up sitting next to an old man from the country who nurses his rough-rolled, black, and crooked tabacos all the way to Havana, never once thinking that the thick blue smoke might intrude on anyone else's comfort.

It is not at all surprising that tobacco is so much a part of Cuban life. It is indigenous to the island. The Indians cultivated it, made cigars out of it, and ground it into powder that they would smoke in pipes, inhaling through their nostrils instead of through their mouths. It is appropriate that the most famous brand of Cuban cigars is therefore called Cohiba, because that is what the Indians called tobacco.

Columbus and his men took the leaf back to Europe and it quickly spread, causing controversy from the beginning. King James of England published *Counterblaste to Tobacco*, in which he criticized smoking, and a Spanish moralizer named Quevado pushed his

A TRIP THROUGH THE CALM AND EXCEEDINGLY BEAUTIFUL PROVINCE OF PINAR DEL RIO OFFERS WELCOME RELIEF FROM THE RUN-DOWN AND CHAOTIC ATMOSPHERE OF HAVANA. MANY SOPHISTICATED HABANEROS DON'T APPRECIATE THE PROVINCE, DISMISSING IT AS A SIMPLE, DULL BACKWATER.

THE PARTAGAS FACTORY IN HAVANA PRODUCES FINE CIGARS FOR EXPORT AROUND THE WORLD. MANY BOXES FIND THEIR WAY TO THE STREETS OF HAVANA, WHERE BLACK MARKET HUSTLERS SELL THEM TO TOURISTS AT A DISCOUNT.

HOW TO SMOKE A GOOD CIGAR

To an aficionado, a good cigar offers as many opportunities for aesthetic pleasure—and even outright snobbery—as a bottle of French wine. And just as with wine drinking, there are rituals to cigar smoking that are said to enhance the experience.

Begin by rolling the cigar lightly between your index finger and thumb, examining the color and suppleness of the wrapper, the shape and solidity of the cigar, and the aroma of the tobacco. Now you are ready to get down to business.

Cheap cigars have holes punched in their tips, or awkward plastic holders for drawing the smoke into your mouth. Good cigars, the kind found in humidors or brought to your table in Parisian restaurants, do not feature any such thing. You need to cut a portion of the tip off, preferably with the small pincer blades of a cigar cutter, to expose the hole through which you will draw the smoke. If you are skilled enough with your hands, you can pinch it off with a sharp fingernail. Biting the cigar tip off with your teeth is so imprecise a method that it is not recommended unless you have no alternative. (However, some would argue that sharp teeth are better than pocket knives, which can mutilate the tip.) If the cigar is dry, wet the end of it with your saliva before cutting it. Don't ever cut too much, or the cigar will draw hot and bitter smoke and you will be forced to work hard pretending you are enjoying the experience.

Lighting a cigar is not as simple as lighting a cigarette. Have a few wooden matches ready, because sometimes it takes more than one to get a cigar going. (Use a lighter if you must, but avoid butane and other substances that will influence the flavor of the smoke.) At one time people heated their cigars before lighting them to burn away the noxious gums used to hold the wrappers in place, but this practice hasn't been necessary since new fixatives were developed a century ago. So, don't pass your cigar above a flame; instead, roll the tuck, or open end, of the cigar a couple of turns just above the reach of the medium-strength flames of a match, to make it draw well. Then stick the stogie in your mouth and light it, using small, even puffs, always making sure the tuck never touches the flame. When you have a red rim and an even burn, blow out the match.

Smoke slowly and never inhale. Let the rich smoke roll thickly in your mouth. Keep it there for a few seconds and savor the variety of tastes and sensations. Blow out the smoke and rest, holding the cigar in your fingers, parallel to the ground. Smoked properly, for maximum enjoyment, a six-inch (15cm) -long cigar might last you almost an hour, puffed once a minute or so.

The ash of a good cigar can be beautiful in a mysterious, gray way, but contrary to popular superstition there is no reason not to flick it off the end of the cigar every once in a while. The ash doesn't affect the flavor. Let it grow, or let if fall, according to your desire. The same holds true for the cigar band. Keep it on if you like it, take if off if you don't; either way, it won't affect the flavor.

You may set your cigar down in an ashtray but you must never stub it out or you'll ruin it. Let it die out on its own and you will have the opportunity to relight it with pleasure (although if a cigar is over half-smoked, a true aficionado would probably light up a fresh one). To relight a cigar, first prepare it by scratching the burnt end with the back end of a wooden match to rough it up. Then light it in the same way you did the first time.

When you finish your cigar, dispose of it discreetly, if possible, so the remains, which even true aficionados admit can smell bad, won't be disagreeable. Then rinse your mouth out with tea or brandy or something else that you like and let the pleasure of the cigar linger in your memory. Soon you may decide to have another.

view that tobacco was destined to be a great scourge for the Spanish. Still, smoking became popular, and in 1850 the Spanish, seeing a potentially huge market for the stuff, began cultivating tobacco in Cuba.

From the beginning there were problems in the trade, as the crown insisted on controlling price, quantity, and the terms of delivery. The growers, wanting a freer market, continually resisted the crown. In fact, the first uprisings against the Spanish were by tobacco growers who were dissatisfied with the system. Tobacco production continued to increase because it was a great crop—cheap to produce, easy to cultivate, and lightweight and easy to transport. And, of course, it was much in demand.

The Spanish controlled the sale of tobacco from the Americas until 1763, when the British occupied Havana and developed a taste for cigars. Then when

MUCH OF THE BEST TOBACCO IS GROWN ON SMALL, FAMILY-RUN FARMS. HERE, A FARMER INSPECTS SOME RECENTLY HARVESTED LEAVES (RIGHT). THE RAREST AND MOST EXPENSIVE TOBACCOS ARE GROWN UNDER MUSLIN TENTS (OPPOSITE PAGE), WHICH SHIELD THE PLANTS FROM EXCESSIVE AMOUNTS OF SUN, WIND, AND RAIN.

the French invaded Spain in 1803, the habit of smoking Cuban cigars spread around the world. As the U.S. market grew, Spain began to fear that plantation owners in the southern states would get together with Cuban cigar growers and makers and cause trouble. To prevent this, Spain again enacted trade restrictions, starting in about 1830. This only further alienated the tobacco growers, who began to support annexationists in the United States who wanted Cuba to become a state.

This political involvement on the part of the tobacco industry continued to grow, fostered to a great degree by the practice of having *lectores,* or "readers," in every cigar and cigarette factory. These readers, first introduced in the mid-nineteenth century, are still integral to the process of making a cigar. They sit at raised desks in the front of the factory and read to the workers as they roll the cigars. In the morning the workers might hear excerpts from the newspaper, learning about the world. In the afternoon they might listen to a novel, a history book, or a political tract. José Martí saw readers as being educators for liberty, and they certainly played a role in the wars for independence.

By the time Céspedes freed his slaves and started the Ten Years' War, tobacco growers were among the most politically sophisticated people in Cuba. The cigar industry had created a small middle class of workers who had risen from poverty under a paternal work system in the countryside to a more impersonal factory environment in the cities, especially in Havana. Unions were organized. Newspapers for cigar workers started up, and, because of the lectores, even illiterate cigar workers were well-informed—and therefore dangerous to Spanish rule.

The Spanish response to Céspedes' revolutionary movement was brutal and swift, and by September 1869 two thousand people lined the docks in Havana awaiting passage out of the country. Many of them were tabaqueros, and most of them went to Key West, which overnight became a major producer of marvelous smokes made from Cuban tobacco by Cuban workers. Key West was closer to Havana than to the U.S. mainland, and in many ways was a world unto itself, apart from Florida. The newly arrived Cubans had no trouble keeping their customs and remaining loyal to their island. They supported Céspedes and his men to the end of the failed Ten Years' War.

Before the second revolution in 1895, Martí and others traveled back and forth between Key West and New York raising money and people's awareness. It is said that the order to launch this second (and successful) war for independence was written on a piece of paper and rolled into a cigar in Key West, before being sent to the revolutionary leaders in Havana.

☰ SENSITIVE FARMERS OF THE VUELTA ABAJO

The best tobacco in the world comes from the Vuelta Abajo, in the province of Pinar del Río, west of Havana. The best tobacco in the Vuelta comes from the area around San Juan y Martínez. This area was first settled in the early 1700s by tobacco growers who were trying to avoid the crown's tobacco monopoly restrictions.

This area has long been a quiet, peaceful part of Cuba, and *Habaneros* still think the people who live here are hicks. "There's nothing to do in Pinar del Río," a city slicker might tell you. Certainly there isn't much night life or excitement, but the scenic beauty of the farms in the Vuelta Abajo and the intriguing caves, rocks, and towering, weathered hills covered with pine trees around Viñales make up for the lack of entertainment.

The tobacco fields are not grand; they are split into small, manageable plots that a family can maintain. This is important because tobacco is a sensitive crop and requires a delicate touch that a large operation might not be able to maintain. Slaves were never a huge part of the tobacco plantations because the very nature of their servitude made it less likely that they would go the extra mile to raise a good crop. Most of the workers over the centuries were freemen.

YOUNG TOBACCO PLANTS POKE OUT OF RICH SOIL IN FRONT OF A TOBACCO-DRYING SHED
IN THE VUELTA ABAJO. THESE SHEDS ARE ESSENTIAL TO CURING TOBACCO PROPERLY, AND WHILE THEY LOOK SIMPLE,
THEY ARE CAREFULLY DESIGNED TO TAKE ADVANTAGE OF THE WIND AND THE SUN.

A TABAQUERO TRIMS THE END OF A CIGAR HE HAS JUST MADE FOR
THE DOMESTIC MARKET (ABOVE). MANY WORKERS PUFF ON THEIR OWN CIGARS
AS THEY WORK. TOBACCO LEAVES DRY IN A SHED (BELOW). THE LEAVES GO
THROUGH SEVERAL STAGES OF DRYING, CURING, AND FERMENTING
BEFORE THEY ARE READY TO BE MADE INTO CIGARS.

Tobacco is planted in November, in stages, so that the plants in different sections of the same field will be ready for harvest at different times. The *veguero,* or "farmer," walks through the field putting down fresh seed or seedlings by hand. The bright green plants spring up from the dark soil a few weeks later in neat rows, the plots broken up here and there by drying sheds. Some of the plants are grown in full sunlight, and others are covered by enormous cheesecloth tents, or *tapados,* that allow only delicate amounts of light and wind to reach the plants.

The leaves from these protected plants are often used as the *capa,* or "wrapper," for fine cigars. Without one of these good satiny, oily wrappers, a cigar just isn't a good cigar. As the plants mature, flowers are pinched off to prevent seeds from forming and to keep the plant's juices flowing. A full-grown plant will stand about five feet (1.5m) tall after three months.

Each plant has about sixteen leaves, which are picked by hand, two or three at a time, starting at the base of the plant. The location of the leaf on the plant has a real effect on its taste and determines the type of cigar it goes into. The higher leaves are generally stronger. The quality of the leaf is also greatly influenced by the weather. A perfect season will offer warm days, cool nights, and no rain, so that the veguero has to water the plants when they are dry.

Since not every year is a good year, aficionados rate the year a cigar was made, much as an oenophile will rate a French wine according to the year it was bottled. Here is what a veguero sees in a tobacco plant.

≋ ≋ ≋

Corona are the leaves high up on the plant that give a cigar strength.

Centro fino are the leaves close to the center of the plant, nearer the stalk, and are always harvested last. They add body and strength to a cigar. Along with the corona, the centro fino are used on the inside of hand-rolled cigars.

Centro gordo are the leaves in the middle of the tobacco plant, often used as capa to wrap the cigar and give it a distinctive, rich aroma.

Volado are the leaves at the bottom of the plant, the *hojas de combustíon,* which are rolled under the capa to help the cigar burn evenly.

≋ ≋ ≋

The harvesting can start as early as January, but most of the leaves are picked between March and April. Each type of leaf must be cured separately.

The first step in the curing process, which changes leaves from green to a silky, oily brown with the feel of a chamois cloth, is to put the leaves in direct sun for several days. Then the leaves, which are usually about eighteen inches (45.7cm) long and several inches wide, are draped over wooden poles,

---

A SELECTION OF CUBAN CIGARS. COHIBAS, WHICH COME IN SEVERAL WIDTHS AND LENGTHS, ARE AMONG THE FINEST CUBAN CIGARS AVAILABLE.

like towels over a towelrack, in drying sheds. These *casas de tabaco* are large, well-ventilated buildings that are usually built on an east-west axis to take advantage of the sun's movement across the sky. In this way the farmers know almost exactly how much sun and air passes through the slat-wood sides and the thatched roofs of the barns and over the drying leaves of tobacco. This part of the cure takes about forty-five days.

When the leaves are dry they are stacked in large piles in warehouses, where the weight of the other leaves and

the heat and humidity cause them to start fermenting. As the center of the pile gets too hot (from the same process that makes a compost heap heat up) the pile is rearranged and restacked. The leaves ferment for another thirty-five days or so, and in this time they lose many impurities, including some tar, nicotine, and oils. Then the leaves are packed up in bales, wrapped in burlap, and left to mellow for up to two years.

final fermentation has cleansed the leaves they are bundled and wrapped in palm bark and aged for as long as two or three more years. Finally, they are taken to one of the big factories in Havana, such as H. Upmann (which makes many cigars for export from its old building near the Capitolio), or to a place like the Francisco Donatién Cigar Factory in Pinar del Río, which concentrates more on the domestic market.

At the factory a *rezagado,* or "grader," sorts the leaves by strength and color (except for leaves that are to be used for an exceptionally fine—and expensive—type of cigar, such as a Cohiba. The leaves for these cigars are fermented and aged at the factory yet a third time, for another two years.) The graders are perhaps the most skilled people in the entire process of making a cigar. They comb through the cured leaves deciding which leaf should go into which type of cigar, based on color, feel, and smell. The color variations are very subtle: *claros* (clears), *colorado-claros* (red-clears), *colorado maduros* (red ripe leaves), *ligeros* (lights), *secos* (dries), *finos* (fines), *amarillos* (yellows), *manchados* (bleeding colors), *quebrados* (broken colors), and more. The best graders can actually recognize between seventy and eighty different colors and combinations.

The graded leaves are given to a blender, who mixes the various grades according to recipes for each type of cigar. Then the tobacco goes into the production room that is thick with the heavy smell of cured tobacco. Smoke rises from fresh cigars in every corner of the room, because the workers are allowed to smoke as much as they want on the job (they may take one cigar home at night, too). Each *tabaquero,* or "roller," is given enough tobacco mixture at the begining of a work day to roll ninety-two cigars. This is a good output,

(The leaves are still a long way from being cigars, a process that has eighty distinct steps.)

Next, a *despalillo* strips the "spine" from each leaf and sorts the leaves roughly according to color. They are fermented again for a month or so to get rid of more impurities. When this

THIS BILLBOARD (ABOVE) READS "HAVANA CIGARS: CUBA, HOME OF THE BEST TOBACCO IN THE WORLD." NEW GROWTH (OPPOSITE) ON THE LANDSCAPE OF PINAR DEL RIO.

© Marc PoKempner

MUCH OF THE WORK IN RURAL CUBA IS STILL DONE WITH ANIMALS, AND THE ROADS HAVEN'T CHANGED MUCH IN CENTURIES. HERE, A FARMER LEADS A TEAM OF PACK MULES THROUGH A CLUSTER OF SMALL HOUSES.

although some of the rollers make 150 or more in a day. The tabaqueros and tabaqueras (since Castro took power, women have taken jobs in the factories) work two to a table in row after row in long, loftlike rooms. Their most important tool is their *chaveta,* the rounded knife used to cut leaves, trim wrappers, and smooth the leaves out for rolling (and to bang out a welcome on the table whenever a visitor is introduced to the room by the lector).

They begin making a cigar by taking a handful of leaves and rolling them inside the *hoja de fortaleza,* which gives the cigar strength. This bunch is then rolled into the *hoja de combustion,* which makes it burn evenly. Then the rough-looking cigar is put into a wooden mold that holds ten or so embryonic cigars. The mold is stacked with several others in a press that is screwed down and left in place for fifteen or twenty minutes to give the cigars good, solid shapes. Then the all-important capa is wrapped around the cigar and sealed with a glue made in Switzerland (from pine trees that do not grow in Cuba). The ends are trimmed with the chaveta, and the tabaquero begins another cigar. Rolling cigars is not easy. Each factory has its own school, and it takes nine months to train a new worker to successfully roll even the simplest shapes.

The stack of cigars is sent to the grading department, where a worker sorts them according to shape and color and passes them on to someone whose job is to secure an *anillo,* or "band," around the end of each cigar to identify it. These workers' movements are peculiar, shaped by the repetitive nature of their job. They rock back and forth and twitch to a silent rhythm as they wrap band after band on thousands of cigars a day, touching the ends of each with a spot of glue. Once banded, the cigar goes in a pinewood box. Finally, an inspector carefully looks over each box of cigars to make sure that everything is right. This strict quality control is essential, because Cuban cigars are important to a lot of people. (John F. Kennedy showed his priorities when he made certain that he had a good supply of H. Uppman cigars before proceeding with his plans during the Cuban Missile Crisis.) Smokers from all over the world will travel an extra mile to find a fine, pure Habano cigar. The considerable reputation enjoyed by fine Cuban cigars is something that transcends politics and feuds, and the Cubans guard that reputation carefully.

CHAPTER SIX

LA HABANA

THE NIGHTTIME VIEW OF HAVANA HINTS AT THE CARIBBEAN SPLENDOR THAT IS THE CITY'S BACKDROP.

Havana is a city of memories. The streets of Habana Vieja, the old city, evoke images of the early conquistadores preparing to leave to conquer the Aztecs; pirates and rebellious slaves fighting the authorities on the waterfront; the Spanish governor and his entourage passing noisily along the Malecón in guarded carriages. The royal palms on the plazas and spreading laurel trees along the boulevards have given shade to lovers, hustlers, and old men quietly passing the tropical afternoons for centuries. Revolutionaries in green fatigues, dancers in sparkling costumes, foreign sailors in neat blue uniforms, and artists, intellectuals, and gangsters in white linen have all left their mark on this hauntingly beautiful city. The majority of the buildings are decaying now after three decades of socialist neglect, but it seems that no amount of crumbling plaster, mildewed walls, and unpolished marble is able to diminish the grandeur of La Habana, as Cubans call it.

Havana owes its greatness to the ships that have been drawn to its wonderful harbor over the centuries, although the early Spanish explorers made two attempts to establish a community before settling on the city's present location. Velázquez founded Villa de San Cristóbal de la Habana in a swamp in 1514, but within just a few years the land proved to be too unstable and fetid for a good settlement. A site

Both photos: © Marc PoKempner

MANY BUILDINGS IN OLD HAVANA ARE UNDERGOING PAINSTAKING RESTORATIONS, BUT OTHERS ARE
MERELY PATCHED TOGETHER WITH WHATEVER MATERIALS ARE AT HAND (OPPOSITE PAGE). A VIEW OF THE HAVANA
SKYLINE FROM THE VEDADO SECTION (ABOVE).

at the mouth of the Almendares river was chosen next, but that also proved to be too swampy. It wasn't until 1519 that the protected and deep harbor that now services ships from all over the world was chosen.

Habana Vieja grew from this first settlement, and this neighborhood, with its colonial architecture and narrow streets built for horse-drawn carriages, is today the most interesting part of Havana. The city at large has spread for miles, in a charming hodgepodge of twentieth-century buildings, but Habana Vieja remains the romantic heart of the city.

The old city is still defined by the eastern edge of the harbor and the limits of a defensive wall that was built in the sixteenth century and torn down in the nineteenth century. Within this neighborhood, which UNESCO has designated a world heritage sight, are 908 historically important buildings: 101 are from the twentieth century; 463 are from the nineteenth century; 200 are from the eighteenth century; and 144 were built in the sixteenth and seventeenth centuries.

With help from UNESCO, the Cuban government has been restoring some of the buildings, especially around the Plaza de Armas. Here, under the comforting shade of a broad, bulbous tree whose rootlike branches make it look almost as though it had grown upside down, is where it all began.

The first mass in Havana was said in the shade of that native ceiba tree near the harbor, and this spot is now celebrated as the founding point of Havana. Though the original tree died long ago, a ceiba still stands, this one planted in 1959. These peculiar trees are considered magical in Cuba, and are sacred to the followers of Santería, the African-based religion that is so common among Cubans. People surreptitiously bury coins and fruits and other offerings in the soil at the base of this ceiba for good—and bad—wishes to come true. On November 16, when the founding of the city is commemorated, people come from far away to walk around the tree three times in a ritual that dates far back into history.

Just behind the tree is a neoclassical jewel called the Templete, a small marble monument with an open room fronted by six columns. The Templete was built in 1827 to house a triptych painted by the French artist Jean Baptiste Vermay. One panel depicts the first mass. Another is of the first town meeting. The third shows the inauguration of the Templete itself. Vermay is buried below the marble floor.

Across the Plaza de Armas from the Templete is one of the oldest structures in Havana, El Castillo de la Fuerza Real, built in 1538 following a brutal pirate attack on Havana. Though it must have had a fierce presence in its day, this small fortress now seems almost quaint.

Children gather on the wall to throw rocks in the fetid green water of the moat, and men train their dogs on the grass in front. The drawbridge is now permanently lowered, a result of the changes that occurred in Havana over the years as it moved from a city under siege to become, along with Lima and Mexico City, one of the jewels of the Spanish empire.

Not too long after the castle was completed, Havana began to take shape as a city. The world was reacting to the chaotic design, or lack of design, of medieval towns in Europe, and Havana, with infusions of the incredible riches flowing out of the New World, was developing as one of the first modern cities. A milestone occurred when the Zanja Real, or "royal ditch," was built in the late sixteenth century to carry clean water from springs outside of Havana to a spigot on the corner near where the cathedral now stands, making life much easier for the city dwellers. (In some ways, however, little has changed for residents of Habana Vieja since the Zanja Real was built; many still depend on water trucks, and haul the water to their apartments on the upper floors of buildings with buckets at the end of ropes.)

Thoughtful planning and amenities like the Zanja Real helped Havana grow in a very civilized manner. It became one of the first cities to reflect the new idea of having an ordered grid of streets that led into plazas and boulevards with

© Marc PoKempner

broad, parklike areas. These public places were essential to making the whole design humanistic. They drew people into the city, and gave the newly arrived settlers a sense of security in a strange world. The result is that although the streets are narrow and the buildings are crowded together (and usually lack adequate plumbing and elec-

THE HOUSES ARE CROWDED TOGETHER IN OLD HAVANA AND THERE ARE FEW OPEN SPACES. HERE, CHILDREN PLAY IN A STREET LINED WITH RUSSIAN AUTOMOBILES AND THE UBIQUITOUS SIGNS OF RESTORATION, REPAIR, AND EMERGENCY MAINTENANCE.

trical wiring) the layout of Habana Vieja is simple and clean. It is difficult to get lost in the old city, even when the streets are at their most chaotic, with children playing baseball, laundry fluttering on balconies, bicycles speeding past, and trucks delivering goods on streets that were meant for horses rather than automobiles.

Both photos: © Richard Riddell

≋ A CITY OF STONE

The buildings of Old Havana are remarkable for the variety of architectural styles they reflect. A striking fact of Havana is that even though it is a tropical city, many of the buildings are made of heavy stone. There is very little of the temporary type of architecture that you find in most tropical cities, with houses made of bamboo and wood that are meant to be rebuilt after fierce storms or too much wear and tear. Havana is solid, even after crumbling through more than three decades of neglect.

One of the most beautiful buildings is the Palacio de los Capitanes Generales (Palace of the Captains General), where the governors sent from Spain lived. Now the wonderful Museum of the City of Havana, this building has been completely restored and offers a startling look into the luxuries that wealthy Cubans took for granted early in the country's history. Sitting

FADING COLORS AND GRAND COLUMNED WALKWAYS EVOKE MEMORIES OF BETTER DAYS PAST FOR THE BUILDINGS ALONG THE MALECON IN OLD HAVANA (LEFT). HAVANA BUILDINGS ARE KNOWN FOR THEIR BALCONIES (OPPOSITE PAGE), WHICH ARE USED AS LIVING ROOMS, LAUNDRY ROOMS, AND EVEN CHICKEN COOPS.

All photos: © Nancy Stout

THESE TWIN HOUSES IN HAVANA (OPPOSITE PAGE) ARE GHOSTS FROM THE TURN OF THE CENTURY, WHEN MONEY POURED INTO THE COUNTRY FROM ABROAD. THE ATTENTION CUBANS HAVE PAID OVER THE CENTURIES TO PURELY DECORATIVE DETAILS IN PUBLIC PLACES IS ASTOUNDING, AS SHOWN IN THIS BRIGHT COLUMN (ABOVE, LEFT) ON A STREET IN HAVANA. A WALK THROUGH ANY CITY IN CUBA WILL REVEAL MANY EXAMPLES OF MARVELOUS TILEWORK (ABOVE, RIGHT), OFTEN IN UNEXPECTED PLACES, SUCH AS ALONG THE BOTTOM OF A STORAGE-ROOM WALL OR LINING THE SIDES OF A DRIVEWAY.

on one of the marble or iron benches under a royal palm tree in the Plaza de Armas it is hard to imagine what life was like in such a grand palace. Built on the site of Havana's first church, this baroque wonder is fronted by a series of high arcades held up by ten Ionic columns, each topped with the Spanish coat of arms done in marble. Inside are beautiful stained glass windows and rooms filled with period furniture and artwork. There is even a bronze eagle that in the 1958 revolution was toppled from its perch above a monument along the Malecón built to honor the men who died on the U.S.S. Maine.

The courtyard of the two-story building is lush, with tropical plants growing up from the cobblestones and a statue of Christopher Columbus reaching for the sky. Cuba's oldest monument is on a wall here, a marble marker carved with the image of a cross and an angel's head. This marks the spot where Doña María de Cepero y Nieto was killed in 1557, felled by a shot (from a harquebus) that was intended for someone else while she was saying her prayers in the chapel.

The cathedral is not far from the Plaza de Armas. Built in 1704, this squat and ungainly building looks as though the large stones used to build it were chosen for their lack of delicacy. But the facade is ornamented with baroque flourishes that have impressed many people over the years, including the

Cuba-Havana- The Maine Monument   P.521

THIS MONUMENT TO THE *U.S.S. MAINE* WAS TOPPLED IN THE 1958 REVOLUTION.

great Cuban writer Alejo Carpentier, who wrote that the outside of the Havana cathedral was like music turned to stone.

The oldest house in Havana, built sometime in the sixteenth century, is close by on Calle Obispo. It is a plain building, although its tiled roof and wooden balconies reflect the Moorish influences that arrived from southern Spain. All of the surviving sixteenth-century houses in Cuba are modest, which reflects the uncertainties of the time. It is easy to forget that Cuba was the New World then, an unknown quantity. The first Spanish inhabitants faced tremendous threats from buccaneers, Indian and slave uprisings, and attacks from for-

eign navies. It is not surprising that the early buildings were simply ornamented.

Out of this defensive posturing came the defining structure of old Havana, which, sadly, no longer exists. Even after several forts were built in the sixteenth century, the city government didn't feel adequately protected against raiders, and insisted that all the residents of Havana contribute slave labor and money to build a protective wall. This forced tribute was not appreciated, and some sections of the wall were poorly built. By 1740, the outside edge of the city, roughly corresponding with the avenue called El Prado today, was ringed with a high stone wall. To top it off, a chain was strung across the harbor entrance at

© D.E. Cox

night to keep invaders away. First it was made of bronze, but this proved to be unwieldy, and later it was made of logs.

Curiously, all this protection wasn't enough to keep the British from sacking and occupying the city for a year in 1762. The economy improved greatly under the British system of free trade, and continued to be good after they traded Havana for Florida. Following the British occupation, Havana experienced a building boom that changed the face of the city with the addition of many beautiful new buildings and parks.

About this time the city architects worked to define the Plaza de Armas more clearly, and the walkways and surrounding buildings haven't changed much since. The Palacio de los Capitanes Generales, the cathedral, and the city's first theater went up. Coffee was coming into importance by the end of the centu-

THE BAROQUE CATHEDRAL OF HAVANA WAS COMPLETED IN 1777. COUPLES OFTEN GET MARRIED AT PUBLIC WEDDING PALACES, ALTHOUGH IN THE YEARS SINCE THE REVOLUTION, FEWER AND FEWER COUPLES HAVE BOTHERED TO LEGALLY TIE THE KNOT.

© Ernesto Bazan

ry and the first cafe was built in Havana, inaugurating a serious national coffee habit that endures to this day.

Finally giving up the idea of containing Havana within the wall, the city built the Prado at the edge of town. Modeled after the Prado in Madrid, this avenue, with its wide, tiled walkway, runs a mile from the sea almost to the Capitolio, the old congress building. Built in the early 1900s, the Capitolio is modeled after the U.S. Capitol in Washington. While many of the buildings that border the Prado have fallen into ruin, the park is still magnificent and popular, especially because of the shade offered by its spreading laurels. Bronze lions mark the entrance to the promenade, and at one spot there is a tree planted in soil that was brought from every country in the Americas. Overlooking the tree is the Aldama mansion, a neoclassical palace that many consider to be Havana's most magnificent home. Nearby is the Palacio de las Bodas (Wedding Palace), where Cubans go to take their vows and pose for photographs. These ceremonies, which take place one after another on Saturdays and Sundays, offer moments of color and joy against the faded grey elegance of contemporary Havana.

About the same time the Prado was constructed, many new elaborate homes, some with several inner courtyards, were built. Churches sprang up with high belfries that served as neighborhood landmarks. Much of the building followed plans based on ideas drafted by a fourteenth-century Franciscan monk named Exemenic. The imposing García Lorca theater was built in 1837 to accommodate ballet and opera productions, making it the largest theater in the Americas. Gradually, Havana became one of the most elegant cities in the New World.

⧫ DISTINCTIVE CUBAN ARCHITECTURE

The city walls were torn down in 1863, and as Havana began to grow farther away from its center the baroque styles and Cuban adaptations to climate that make the city so distinctive spread. Stone buildings were everywhere, built with patios, red-tile roofs similar to those in Andalusia, and elaborate baroque facades.

The houses of the old city are distinctive for their huge front doors, called *portales*. As tall as fifteen feet (4.6m) and made of wood with heavy brass lugs holding them together, they would seem to offer sufficient protection against battering rams, tanks, and small bombs, and no doubt some of them have served this purpose over the years. They were built large enough to allow carriages to pass through and into the courtyard where the storage rooms are. These portales, which are still very much in use, have smaller doors built into them to admit pedestrians. Built into these small doors

© Marc PoKempner

are even smaller hatches, often covered with grillwork. Called *postigos*, they are situated at head height and are useful for gossiping with neighbors and for checking out visitors before allowing them to enter.

The ground floors of these houses were originally intended for business and storage, with slaves and servants living in low-ceilinged *entresuelos* between the storerooms and the mezzanine, where the family lived. The family rooms

designing a house: letting in light and air, and keeping out the heat and the blinding sun. Vitrales—called *lucetas* when they are rectangular and *mediopuntos* when shaped like half-moons—are found all over the country and it is difficult not to be cheered up by the light pouring through purple and red and yellow and green glass and dancing in these colors across the walls.

There are many other wonderful architectural details common to Cuban buildings that serve primarily to keep air and light at the best levels: small transoms, which are also called postigos, found at the top of high doors; *mamparas*, huge hand-carved double doors between rooms; *rejas*, window grills made of wood (in the very old buildings and in the country) or iron that keep intruders out when the windows are open; and large, Moorish-style patios, with wells, fountains, and lush plants that keep the house cool and sometimes even provide fruit for the table.

The interiors of the buildings built before the twentieth century were often designed with high white walls, dark wood moldings, and lots of marble, either from Italy or from Cuba's Isla de Los Piños (now called Isla de la Juventud). Shuttered windows were common then, as were rocking chairs. In the nineteenth century, most houses had at least one *candela*, or bowl with a live coal in it, for guests who wished to light their cigars.

© Richard Riddell

COURTYARDS (OPPOSITE PAGE) ARE USUALLY SHARED BY SEVERAL FAMILIES. THIS BUILDING (ABOVE) HAS UNDERGONE A SECURE, IF NOT FLATTERING, RESTORATION. THESE SCENES ARE TYPICAL OF HAVANA, A CITY IN NEED OF A LOT OF PAINT, PLASTER, AND TWO-BY-FOURS.

upstairs often had marble floors, high ceilings, and huge louvered doors with colored glass windows set above or into them. These *vitrales* are one of the most distinctive and charming features of Cuban architecture.

Made of colored glass, vitrales fulfilled one of the two main goals the early Cuban architects considered when

Opposite page © Marc PoKempner Both photos this page: © Richard Riddell

THE MAGNIFICENT STONE BUILDINGS OF HAVANA BOAST SOME OF THE WORLD'S MOST IMPRESSIVE EUROPEAN FACADES, COMPLETE WITH SMALL BALCONIES LIKE THESE (OPPOSITE PAGE). THIS GRAND OLD THEATER (LEFT) IS TYPICAL OF THE BUILDINGS NEAR THE HOTEL INGLATERRA. OPEN DOORS ALONG THE PRADO IN HABANA VIEJA REVEAL MANY ARCHITECTURAL WONDERS, FOR INSTANCE THIS SWEEPING MARBLE STAIRCASE (BELOW).

© Richard Riddell

**SEVERAL EXQUISITELY RESTORED
PHARMACIES ARE OPEN IN
THE BLOCKS SURROUNDING THE
PLAZA DE ARMAS. HERBS, HOMEO-
PATHIC MEDICINES, AND PHARMACEU-
TICALS ARE FOR SALE IN THESE
CHARMING SHOPS.**

to the Casa de Infusiones (House of Infusions), which offers traditional Cuban drinks made with fresh chamomile, orange rind, vanilla, sweet basil, oregano, linden, and anise, among other unusual flavors. Of course, they also serve very strong Cuban coffee. And it wouldn't be too difficult to find a little glass of rum if you happened to be in the mood for refreshment of a different nature.

As you sip your drink, think about the street names of old Havana. Many of them have a story to tell.

≋ ≋ ≋

Calle Refugio (Refuge Street) is so-named because a nineteenth-century governor named Mariano Rocafort took refuge in a beautiful widow's house on this street during a severe storm. He ended up staying much longer than the neighbors felt was necessary—long after the rain had passed and the sun had gone down.

Calle O'Reilly was named after a Spanish government man with an Irish name who

The best way to get a good sense of this architecture is to visit one of the eighteenth-century houses open to the public, such as the Casa de Calvo de la Puerta (House of the Bald Door) on Obrapía street in Habana Vieja. This special house has two courtyards, each with verandas all the way around. Almost every room in the house opens onto one patio or another, and a narrow pas-

sageway connects the two patios and the dining room. After leaving the house walk over to Obispo street and have a look at the old pharmacies that sell perfume, medicine, and dried herbs from gleaming glass jars and bottles on the counter. If you are lucky there will be fresh herbs laid out on paper, and the room will be filled with distinctive tropical scents. Or go around the corner

was the first Spanish official to enter Havana after the British traded the city to Spain in return for the territory of Florida in 1763.

Calle Tejadillo (Tile Street) was so-called because the first house to have a tile roof was built on this street.

Calle Lamparilla was the first street in the city to have lamps.

≈ THE TWENTIETH CENTURY

Habana Vieja is now only a small section of the city, where sixty thousand people out of a population of two million live. Havana proper now spreads out far beyond the boundaries of the old wall, and while much of the city is made up of repetitive, oppressively dull, poured-concrete highrises, some parts of twentieth-century Havana are fascinating. The old gave way to the new after Cuba won independence from Spain in 1898, and the face of the city changed dramatically. One interesting building is the Hotel Ambos Mundos, on Calle Obispo, right up the street from the ancient pharmacies. This nondescript building is painted pink, except for the white walls outside of the corner room where Ernest Hemingway lived for many years before buying his estate in 1939 on the outskirts of Havana. Hemingway roamed this neighborhood when he fin-

IF YOU LACK ENERGY, PAY A VISIT TO A CAFETERIA FOR A TINY CUP OF CUBAN ESPRESSO, MADE WITH A MACHINE LIKE THE ONE BEHIND THE MAN IN THIS PHOTO.

ished writing for the day, and a few of his local hangouts became known all over the world.

Near Ambos Mundos there is a charming restaurant called La Bodeguita del Medio (The Little Store Halfway Up the Block), which was a bohemian hangout for a long time, a place where Cubans could go to escape the endless parade of tourists that filled the nightclubs and casinos of Havana. Errol Flynn, who lived in Havana for a while, is

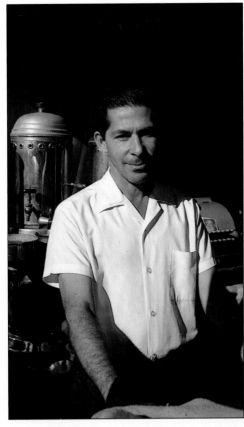

© D. E. Cox

A SMUGGLER'S VIEW OF THE HAVANA WATERFRONT

Hemingway lived in Cuba for many years, and while there are differences of opinion as to how well he spoke Spanish and how well he assimilated himself into Cuban culture, there is no doubt that he was an astute observer. This excerpt from *To Have and Have Not*, a novel about smugglers working the Havana to Key West route early in the century, certainly rings true.

You know how it is there early in the morning in Havana with the bums still asleep against the walls of the buildings; before even the ice wagons come by with ice for the bars? Well, we came across the square from the dock to the Pearl of San Francisco Café to get coffee and there was only one beggar awake in the square and he was getting a drink out of the fountain....

Both photos: © Marc Pokempner

reported to have said that the Bodeguita was the best place in the world to get drunk. The walls are covered with graffiti in many languages, including Russian, Ethiopian, and Portuguese, and the bartenders crank out endless glasses of crushed yerbabuena, rum, soda, and sugar—mojitos.

It is said in Havana that Hemingway once wrote "My Mojito en La Bodeguita, My Daiquiri in El Floridita," and La Bodeguita has several copies of this phrase in Hemingway's handwriting hung behind the bar. It doesn't hurt business when people feel they are sharing something with Papa every time they have a mojito in La Bodeguita. The Hemingway hype is strong in Havana. According to Tom Miller, in his book *Trading with the Enemy*, Papa never said anything about his mojito; he claims the phrase was a public relations gambit thought up soon after the 1958 revolution. If so, it certainly was successful. Tourists continue to come from all over to toast Papa with his favorite drink.

There is no doubt that Hemingway put back more than a few drinks at the Floridita, a restaurant only a few blocks up the hill, but miles away in terms of elegance. The bartenders here wear white shirts, bowties, and red vests, and the expensive dining room has murals on the walls and flowers in crystal set on white tablecloths. Gary Cooper, Tennessee Williams, Ava Gardner, and, of course, Hemingway, all at one time or

RESTAURANTE-BAR
Floridita
LA CUNA DEL DAIQUIRI

TWO OF ERNEST HEMINGWAY'S FAVORITE HANGOUTS, THE BOHEMIAN LA BODEGUITA
DEL MEDIO (OPPOSITE PAGE) AND THE MORE EXCLUSIVE FLORIDITA (ABOVE).

© D. E. Cox

THE FLORIDITA (ABOVE) HAS BEEN CAREFULLY RESTORED TO MAKE IT EASIER FOR TOURISTS TO IMAGINE THAT THEY'RE DRINKING A DAIQUIRI IN THE PRESENCE OF HEMINGWAY'S GHOST, BUT NOT MUCH SPANISH IS SPOKEN HERE — WITH FEW EXCEPTIONS, ONLY FOREIGNERS ARE ALLOWED TO ENTER. MEN PLAY CHECKERS ON THE STREET (BELOW).

© Marc PoKempner

another hung out here eating lobsters and sipping the house drink. Made of lime, shaved ice, rum, and sugar, this powerful drink was invented at the Floridita. The inventor, a bartender named Constante, named it for a small, perfect, crescent-shaped beach near the eastern city of Santiago de Cuba called Daiquiri.

The Floridita is just a few blocks from Centro Habana, the first neighborhood outside the boundaries of the old city wall. Here and there along the Prado, tall marble and stone columns become more and more prevalent as architectural details on the buildings. Distinctly Cuban, these architectural marvels come in all types and sizes— Doric, Corinthian, and Ionic columns are sometimes mixed together on a single building. These columns are often strung together to form lengthy colonnades that offer welcome relief from the city's hot sun and heavy rain.

Centro Habana is a crowded neighborhood of faded pastel buildings, where people lean down from every balcony and life is lived in the calle. Men will gather around a folding table in the street to throw down dominoes and smoke cigars for hours. The neighborhood children play marbles and ride bikes while their parents gossip in the doorways. This neighborhood underwent a boom after the country won independence from Spain, and department stores and hotels and palaces were

LA HABANA ▪ 137

built everywhere. These once-elegant buildings have faded into wrecks, and open entranceways offer glimpses of decaying marble stairways and faded tile-work. Art nouveau details tumble into neoclassical facades and the whole effect is strangely romantic and sad. The atmosphere of Centro Habana is one that hangs in the imagination and constantly draws visitors back for another look.

Abutting Centro Habana is Vedado, the international center of the city, where airlines, government ministries, and hotels—the old Havana Hilton is now the state-run Habana Libre—cater to visitors from all over the world. La Rampa, the popular name for Twenty-third Street, is the crowded business artery of Vedado, and it runs down a small hill (thus its nickname, which means "the ramp") to the sea wall, or Malecón, which is the true soul of Havana.

The Malecón is where you would go if you wanted to meet a lover, a double agent, your mother and her Santería priest, a bicycle repairman, or a Rastafarian selling black market Bob Marley tapes. Everyone passes along this walkway, which follows the crashing sea from La Punta Castle, at the mouth of the harbor, several miles to La Chorrera, a seventeenth-century fortress that has been turned into a restaurant. This fortress, at the mouth of the Alemendares River, is the last stop in

THE RESTORATION OF HABANA VIEJA

Much of Havana has gone unpainted for decades due to lack of money and materials. These years of cosmetic neglect have left Havana so gray and weathered that the sight of a restored house, such as José Martí's bright yellow and green birthplace (now a museum), can be quite a shock. The fresh paint and small, well-tended courtyard of this lovingly restored wooden house seem unbelievably luxurious in comparison to its surroundings.

There are other surprises here and there in Old Havana, thanks to the dedicated efforts of Eusebio Leal Spengler, the city historian and the director of a fifteen-year-old restoration project funded in part by the United Nations Educational, Scientific, and Cultural Organization (UNESCO). The United Nations organization named Old Havana a world heritage sight in 1982. A walk along the cobblestone streets these days requires nimble feet to navigate around the ramshackle wooden buttresses holding up many of the buildings, the piles of gravel, and the workmen putting fresh plaster and paint on colonial treasures. The difficulty of the passage pays off once you reach the Plaza de Armas and stand in the midst of wonderfully restored colonial architectural treasures boasting tile walls, carved stonework, and cool fountains. Occasionally you will see the almost electric color known as Havana blue that was so popular in past centuries.

There are over three thousand historical buildings in the area; by contrast, fewer than one hundred of the most important buildings have been restored. Still, Cubans take great pride in Old Havana, and even though the devastated economy has left architects sometimes unable to find paper on which to draw their plans, and has forced builders to improvise in the face of antiquated electrical systems and shortages of building supplies, the work goes on, *poco a poco*. And the bright colors and clean stone walls help brighten up a city that was once known to sparkle in the light of the Caribbean sun.

© Richard Riddell

Havana proper before you hit Miramar, the neighborhood where many wealthy families owned mansions before Castro took power.

There are usually a few dozen men and boys floating in inner tubes in the water off La Chorrera, fishing lines out to catch a big one. Their inner tubes are invariably wrapped in netting to protect them from being punctured on the sharp rocks of the coastline. Some of these tubes are fitted with oars and oarlocks, and fishermen have been known to float all the way to Florida. Some of these drifting fishermen (or refugees, if you prefer) have been killed by sharks or the weather. The sun and saltwater combine to break down the walls of the inner-tube, and if the currents don't move you quickly enough, you sink before reaching the Florida Keys. Many people over the years have felt that the risks associated with these illegal escapes from Cuba are worth the possible reward of reaching Miami. Still, most of the people you see are just trying to catch a good meal.

LA BODEGUITA DEL MEDIO IS A SCRUFFY PLACE WITH SOME OF THE BEST CUBAN FOOD IN HAVANA. SOME SAY THAT ERNEST HEMINGWAY PREFERRED THE MOJITOS HERE. WHETHER HE DID OR NOT, HIS GHOST LOOMS LARGE.

© Nancy Stout

WHEREVER THERE IS WATER
IN HAVANA THERE ARE MEN
FISHING, AND OFTEN THEY'LL SELL
THEIR CATCH TO PASSING
MOTORISTS. SOMETHING ABOUT
THE MALECON INSPIRES
ROMANCE, AND YOU CAN'T WALK
ALONG IT WITHOUT SEEING
LOVERS EMBRACING.

© Mel Rosenthal

The Malecón is busy twenty-four hours a day, and safe to walk along at almost any hour. At night huge groups of teenagers spill into the roadway, listening to music and chattering about the world. Prostitutes ply their trade along the sidewalks, catering to foreign visitors just as they did in the 1950s. Everyone seems to live and let live along the Malecón; it is a place to sit with a bottle of rum and your friends and play cards on a Friday evening. It is also where you would take your new girlfriend or boyfriend to hold hands and kiss. Your family might walk here after buying ice cream at the huge Coppelia ice cream parlor in Vedado. Visitors look over this wide promenade from their rooms high in the grand Hotel Nacional, and often feel compelled to descend to where the action is. Havana, despite the troubles it has seen over the centuries, remains the focal point of a lively country, full of people who know how to enjoy themselves. Anyone who visits Cuba cannot help but want to be part of the Havana scene. And if you open yourself to it, the city will undoubtedly welcome you.

Both photos: © Ernesto Bazan

A FISHERMAN (OPPOSITE PAGE) HAULS IN A SERIOUS FISH THAT MIGHT MAKE A GOOD MEAL, OR EARN HIM SOME
POCKET MONEY. THIS YOUNG MAN (ABOVE) DISPLAYS HIS CATCH ALONG THE MALECON IN HAVANA,
HOPING TO SELL IT TO A HUNGRY CUSTOMER.

BIBLIOGRAPHY

Bolívar Aróstegui, Natalia. *Los Orishas en Cuba*. La Habana: Ediciones Unión, 1991.

Carbajo, Antonio. *El Millón Catorce de Dicharones Cubanos*. Miami Springs, Florida: Language Research Press, 1968.

Cardenal, Ernesto. *In Cuba*. New York: New Directions, 1974.

Davidoff, Zino. *The Connoisseur's Book of the Cigar*. Translated by Lawrence Grow. New York: McGraw-Hill, 1967.

Evans, Walker. *Havana 1933*. New York: Pantheon Books, 1989.

Gómez, Máximo. *Museo Hemingway*. La Habana: Editorial Letras Cubanas, 1985.

González-Wippler, Migene. *The Santería Experience*. Englewood Cliffs, N.J.: Prentice-Hall, 1982.

Gorgoni, Gianfranco. *Cuba Mi Amor*. Verona, Italy: Parise Press, 1990.

Guillermo, Jorge. *Cuba: Five Hundred Years of Images*. New York: Abaris Books, 1992.

Hartman Matos, Alejandro. *Diario de Navegación (Los días de Colón en Baracoa)*. Guantánamo, Cuba: Ediciones el Mar y la Montaña, 1992.

Hemingway, Ernest. *To Have and Have Not*. New York: Macmillan, 1962.

Lewis, Barry, and Peter Marshall. *Into Cuba*. New York: Alfred van der Marck Editions Inc., 1985.

McManus, Jane. *Getting to Know Cuba*. New York: St. Martin's Press, 1989.

Michener, James A., and John Kings. *Six Days in Havana*. Austin: University of Texas Press, 1989.

Miller, Tom. *Trading with the Enemy: A Yankee Travels through Castro's Cuba*. New York: Atheneum, 1992.

Nuñez Gutiérrez, Miguel Luis. *La Habana: Salas del Museo Nacional de Cuba Palacio de Bellas Artes*. La Habana: Editorial Letras Cubanas, 1990.

Oppenheimer, Andres. *Castro's Final Hour: The Secret Story Behind the Coming Downfall of Communist Cuba*. New York: Simon and Schuster, 1992.

Ripol, Carolos. *José Martí: A Biography in Photographs and Documents*. Coral Gables, Florida: Senda Nueva de Ediciones, 1992.

Sale, Kirkpatrick. *The Conquest of Paradise: Christopher Columbus and the Columbian Legacy*. New York: Alfred A. Knopf, 1990.

Sapieha, Nicolas. *Old Havana, Cuba*. London: Tauris Parke Books, 1990.

Smith, Wayne S. *Portrait of Cuba*. Atlanta: Turner Publishing, 1991.

Westfall, L. Glenn. *Key West: Cigar City U.S.A*. Key West, Florida: The Historic Key West Preservation Board, 1984.

Wurdemann, John G.F. *Notes on Cuba*. New York: Arno Press, 1971 (originally published in 1844).

INDEX